MORE PRAISE FOR
MICROSLICES

We now create more data in a week than existed in the entirety of human history before 1997. With all that data available to us, being able to analyze it isn't just an asset—it's become a necessity. Microslices is a great dive into understanding exactly why the boom in data sciences will completely change the way you use professional services. It's, quite simply, a must-read.

Keith Ferrazzi,
author of Never Eat Alone *and the #1 NY Times*
***bestseller* Who's Got Your Back**

The book provides an excellent view into the future for everyone that provides or utilizes professional services. It predicts the changes coming to the industry and how to embrace the changes in order to increase productivity and profitability. A must-read!

Major General Steven W. Smith (Ret.),
CEO of S.W. Smith & Associates

Microslices provides an insider view from a former CIA analyst on how executives must harness big data into a competitive advantage. A must read for any executive concerned about the accelerating pace of innovation required in the new big data era.

David Niu,
founder and CEO of TINYpulse

Provocative! Microslices interrupts our long-held assumptions about the advice business and helps us better probe the most important question of the day—how do we innovate?

Martha Johnson,
leadership speaker, author, and former administrator of the US General Services Administration (GSA)

This book provides extremely valuable insight on the future of consulting and professional services. It describes the disruptive forces that are currently in play and takes a look at the way work will be performed and why and how firms will be hired by clients in the future. As the managing member of a large CPA firm, I find this book a must-read to help our firm stay ahead of the curve.

John Bly,
CPA, CVA, CM&AA, CVA, and author of *Cracking the Code:*
An Entrepreneur's Guide to Growing Your Business through
Mergers and Acquisitions for Pennies on the Dollar

The consulting market is the largest and last standing that has not been turned upside down by the digital revolution. Microslices speaks directly to this trend and what is already beginning to occur.

Edwin Miller,
founder and CEO of 9Lenses and author of 9Lenses
Insight to Action *and* Snapshot9

This book provides a carefully nuanced look at what the world of consulting will look like ten or more years into the future. A compelling read on how trends in data science and business analytics will change the ways in which businesses will creatively use internal and external expertise to successfully run their enterprises.

Manoj Malhotra,
Jeff B. Bates Professor for the Darla Moore School of
Business and Chairman of the Management Science
Department at the University of South Carolina

If you are in the advice giving or receiving business, this book should be on your must-read-today list. John Dillard pulls no punches in explaining why consulting firms—and the clients who use them—are in big trouble if they don't adapt right now.

John Doerr,
cofounder and president of RAIN Group and bestselling author of Insight Selling: Surprising Research on What Sales Winners Do Differently

Microslices is a provocative look at how digitization of knowledge work and data science will change how enterprises operate and improve over time. John presents an intriguing vision of how these innovations may unfold and criteria to use now in selecting professional services to guide your path there.

Leif C. Ulstrup,
founder and CEO of Primehook Technology, former president of Computer Sciences Corporation (CSC) Federal Consulting, and former principal, Deloitte Consulting

Microslices has changed the way I look at the world of management consulting. As the cofounder of three successful consulting firms, I was especially intrigued by the view into the changing landscape of how our services will be procured and used in the future. There are many extremely good nuggets of information in this easy-to-read book that we are already starting to leverage in my current firm. Thank you John for writing Microslices!

John Miller,
cofounder of The Clearing, former vice president of SRA International, and cofounder of Touchstone Consulting Group

MICROSLICES

MICROSLICES

THE DEATH OF CONSULTING

AND WHAT IT MEANS FOR EXECUTIVES

JOHN M. DILLARD

Advantage®

Published by Advantage, Charleston, South Carolina.
Member of Advantage Media Group.

ADVANTAGE is a registered trademark and the Advantage colophon is a trademark of Advantage Media Group, Inc.

Printed in the United States of America.

ISBN: 978-1-59932-532-3
LCCN: 2015946801

Book design by George Stevens.

This publication is designed to provide accurate and authoritative information in regard to the subject matter covered. It is sold with the understanding that the publisher is not engaged in rendering legal, accounting, or other professional services. If legal advice or other expert assistance is required, the services of a competent professional person should be sought.

Advantage Media Group is proud to be a part of the Tree Neutral® program. Tree Neutral offsets the number of trees consumed in the production and printing of this book by taking proactive steps such as planting trees in direct proportion to the number of trees used to print books. To learn more about Tree Neutral, please visit **www.treeneutral.com**. To learn more about Advantage's commitment to being a responsible steward of the environment, please visit **www.advantagefamily.com/green**

Advantage Media Group is a publisher of business, self-improvement, and professional development books and online learning. We help entrepreneurs, business leaders, and professionals share their Stories, Passion, and Knowledge to help others Learn & Grow. Do you have a manuscript or book idea that you would like us to consider for publishing? Please visit **advantagefamily.com** or call **1.866.775.1696.**

For my wife and daughters.

CONTENTS

PART II: "MICROSLICES" IN ACTION

THE DEATH OF CONSULTING

Why does the word "consultant" conjure up such strong emotions?

S tereotypes, being what they are, are often amusing. But sometimes they bear a nugget of truth. On hearing "consultant," you might picture a trusted advisor who helped you through a tough challenge in your executive career. Or you might picture your worst nightmare: a consulting firm that claimed to have all the answers, only to submit three months of invoices before leaving your organization with vague advice and few solutions. (And you know that a career has established itself in pop culture if there's a cable show about it; Showtime's *House of Lies* is all about consultants who are, presumably, loose with the facts.)

You might not be able to identify a "consultant" very easily, because consultants take on many forms. Leadership coaches, defense contractors, recruiters, investment bankers, accountants, lawyers, and even doctors are, for the purposes of this book, in the consulting business. Consulting goes by many names: contracting, advisory services, coaching, staffing, SETA (systems engineering and technical assistance),[1] counsel, freelancer, and outsourcer are all terms of art one might equate with consulting.

In the end, these "professional services firms" (a term I'll use throughout this book) share one common characteristic: they give advice for a living. Sometimes that advice is sought for something very specialized, sometimes it's for an outside opinion, and sometimes it's just for something you don't have time to mess with. All of those are valid and often valuable uses of consultants.

As an executive, you may have hired a firm or a person to improve a process, to coach your leadership team, to develop a strategy, to analyze product lines, to develop a new pricing strategy, or to build an information system. Similarly, you may have hired a consultant to provide legal advice, review human resources policies, provide people for a call center operation, or provide medical advice and coaching to employees. These are all forms of consultative advice giving, and all face the same opportunities and challenges.

In my own career, I've worked for two of the former "Big Five" (Deloitte, KPMG, Accenture, E&Y, and PwC), an Internet boutique, a government strategy firm, a massive SETA contractor, and my own start-up. Combined, these firms delivered hundreds of thousands of different services for their clients, in hundreds of thousands of different ways, and with hundreds of thousands of employees. But in the end, each simply provided outside advice,

---

1 | SETA contractors are a common variety of consultant in government work, providing augmented staff for underfunded and understaffed agencies.

expertise, and solutions to an executive who needed it. That's the basis of the professional services transaction.

Defined broadly, there are many professions that provide consulting services. A lawyer provides advice to executives on the law. An accountant doles out advice on tax, transactions, and auditing. A government contractor gives advice on technology or policy—or provides an extra pair of hands. Even your family doctor is paid, in part, for her advice. Nurse staffing, insurance companies, stock brokerages, and investment bankers are consultancies in their own way.

I have no doubt insulted every doctor and lawyer who may be reading, but I'm not making that comparison to redefine an industry. I'm presenting the hypothesis that the dynamics affecting consulting will affect all professional services.

> The basic business model of professional services has changed very little in your lifetime.

Most of the traditional consultants I know probably don't like to hear that, but it's well documented.[2] McKinsey & Co. and Booz Allen Hamilton pioneered an approach to providing business advice in the late 1920s. Since then, consulting firms have been providing teams of outside experts to solve problems that a company or a government or an organization can't solve themselves. They typically provide that service for an hourly or daily fee. Sometimes they stick around and

2 | Clayton M. Christensen, Dina Wang, and Derek van Bever, "Consulting on the Cusp of Disruption," *Harvard Business Review*, October 2013.

help implement; sometimes they leave. But the advice-for-hire model hasn't changed a whole lot in nearly a century.

The types of firms providing that advice haven't changed much either. David Maister, one of the most widely admired writers on professional services, classified professional services firms in four groups based on two criteria: (a) the extent of the firm's contact with the client and (b) whether the service is standardized or customized. That neat grouping of four types of firms has held up well for decades. However, this model is turning upside down and inside out, which will become apparent as you read this book.

Consulting Is Dying. Most Consultants Don't Know It

This may sound insane from a guy who owns a company that delivers consulting services, but there's a method to my madness. I am excited, and you should be too. There are a lot of smart people who are working on this problem and creating the next generation of advice giving. We'll outline several cases of those buyers and sellers in this book. But there are many buyers and practitioners who are simply unaware of the change that's happening around them.

The great news in all of this doomsaying is that when something dies, it creates a space for something *new* to emerge. The reason I find that so thrilling—and the reason I wrote this book—is to shine a light on those new ideas and make them accessible to anyone who hires a consultant (or lawyer, accountant, leadership coach, or anyone else who they might pay for advice). Only by adapting this new delivery model will executives who hire professional services firms continue to get the guidance and value that they need.

"Disruption" Isn't New; It's Just New to Consulting

Disruptive innovation is a phrase that every dime-store MBA has dropped into casual conversation at every possible wine and cheese party. It's a widely overused and misused term, and it's certainly not new. It is, however, a new development in professional services.

So what the heck is disruptive innovation? Clayton Christensen, Harvard professor and author of countless books and articles on the subject, most notably *The Innovator's Dilemma*, called it:

> *The phenomenon by which an innovation transforms an existing market or sector by introducing simplicity, convenience, accessibility, and affordability where complication and high cost are the status quo.*[3]

To put it crudely: expensive, complicated stuff sucks. Disruptive innovation fixes it through dramatic and rapid change, often as a result of a new technology, a niche business model, or a cultural shift. You have already watched this happen. Travel agencies. Hard drive manufacturers. Lighting. Cab companies. In fact, one might argue that disruptive innovation is an inevitable consequence of progress and experimentation and that every job and every industry is simply racing against time.

A great example comes from the book I mention above, *The Innovator's Dilemma*,[4] involving the mechanical excavator industry

3 | "Disruptive Innovation," Clayton Christensen Institute, http://www.christenseninstitute.org/key-concepts/disruptive-innovation-2/#sthash.mr4BtlJZ.dpuf.

4 | Clayton Christensen. *The Innovator's Dilemma: When New Technologies Cause Great Firms to Fail (Management of Innovation and Change)*. Harvard Business Review Press; 1997.

(for the layman: steam shovels). Hydraulics used to be a very specialized, weird, niche technology that only worked on a very small scale. Before hydraulics, excavation used coal, then gasoline, to move a cable, which did the work.

Hydraulics got some penetration in a niche, but the big firms didn't invest in that technology because their customers didn't want it, and those firms were trying to serve their customers. After a while, the hydraulics got a little better and a little better, and then—rather suddenly—the tables turned and traditional excavation manufacturers had no chance of catching up. Hydraulics became the norm, and steam and cable–actuated excavators were left in the dust.

Consulting has been insulated from disruptive innovation for a long time, because it's high touch and high trust and can take advantage of technological change by adapting its services to the trends its clients face. Don't get me wrong—consulting has morphed continuously over time. The services that firms perform, and the topics they perform them on, have changed, but the delivery model and economic model of professional services firms has not changed much. Until now.

> This book explains exactly what is driving the change, what will take the current system's place, and what exactly you can do about it.

There is a traditional model of consulting and a new model of consulting. If you get stuck buying traditional consulting, you'll be wasting time and money while your competitors and adversaries adapt by hiring different kinds of firms that deliver new services in different ways. Failure to adapt is not only a competitive misstep; you risk missing opportunities to use data to change your business, to solve problems much more quickly, and to take advantage of hyperspecialized solutions to specialized challenges.

> In short, organizations that don't change the way they buy professional services will receive advice that is data poor, slow, and generic.

This book is written for the executive who buys professional services and for the leader who puts his or her career (or company) on the line to pay a hell of a lot of money for the advice and help of outsiders. If you're one of those people, you're going to get a lot out of this book.

When you finish reading, you're going to understand:

- ○ What "disruptive innovation" means for professional services

- ○ The three driving forces behind that change

- ○ The future delivery model of consulting and professional services

- ○ Why this benefits you, the executive

- ○ Tangible, specific steps you can take to react right now

This book may also be a valuable tool if you are a consultant, lawyer, accountant, or any kind of practitioner of professional services. I hope that it helps you serve your clients better, allowing you to grow, adapt, and innovate. It will help you hire and partner with consultants and allow you and your providers to work together to adapt in an era of disruption and intense innovation.

> Microslices is the inevitable future business model of professional services. It is the accelerating specialization, compression, and automation of consulting activities.

Futurists are fashionable, but they aren't focused on professional services. This book places professional services in the context of futurist thinking. As a result, it is a bit technical at times. Fear not: it's not quite as intense as other books you've read by popular futurists or professors at Singularity University. It does draw on those ideas and applies them to the use of professional services by executives like you.

While I am fascinated by the technical trends shaping our work, know that this book is unlike the in-vogue futurist books you may have seen or read. I am not a computer scientist. I didn't invent the flatbed scanner. I have not designed biomedical nanobots that seek out and destroy cancer cells. I am just a regular guy who happens to be passionate about both professional services and futurist writing. Based on experience and research, I am excited about the future and what it brings to my profession and my clients. That's relevant for this book because those important trends affect how you buy consulting.

Thorough analysis of the future of work has been covered in great books like *The Second Machine Age*,[5] *Exponential Organizations*,[6] and *The Singularity Is Near*.[7] Many of these works paint brilliant pictures of technology and how it's going to change the world. But few can focus on a particular industry, the employees who work in it, and the customers it serves. In this book, I look at the future through the lens of professional services and explore what it means for the industry and its customers.

I don't have a wall full of PhDs, but I do bring a couple of interesting things to the table that give me a unique perspective on this subject.

First, I've spent a career giving advice. My first job, at the CIA, wasn't too different from my job in consulting; I was charged with sifting through mountains of information related to a problem, identifying trends, and communicating that information to decision makers. My first consulting job was with Cambridge Technology Partners, where we did work for Deutsche Bank and Swissair on client/server and e-business technology. I worked for Deloitte Consulting on strategy for state government and automotive. I worked for Red Sky Interactive, which was one of those late 1990s Internet-bubble firms that did a little bit of creative, a little bit of technology, and a little bit of business consulting. I worked for KPMG, in a very classic Big Five/Big Four environment. And finally, I worked for Touchstone

5 | Erik Brynjolfsson and Andrew McAfee, *The Second Machine Age: Work, Progress, and Prosperity in a Time of Brilliant Technologies.* W. W. Norton & Company, 2014.

6 | Salim Ismail; Michael S Malone; Yuri van Geest; Peter H Diamandis, *Exponential organizations: why new organizations are ten times better, faster, and cheaper than yours (and what to do about it).* New York: Diversion Books, 2014.

7 | Ray Kurzweil, *The Singularity Is Near: When Humans Transcend Biology.* Penguin, 2006.

Consulting, later acquired by SRA, which was a strategy firm focused exclusively on federal executives.

I have worked on projects in at least ten different industries solving problems in operations research, human resources, information technology, and human capital. I have founded a successful and respected consulting firm. I've watched how the professionals learn and grow and deliver value to their clients. I know what customers like—and dislike—about consultants.

Calling myself an expert is presumptuous, but I can enthusiastically call myself a student of the professional services industry and of the future. I have devoted my career to understanding the business of advice giving and the trends shaping that industry.

Second, I have retained the pattern recognition mindset of a CIA intelligence analyst. The best thing about cutting your teeth at the CIA doesn't have a thing to do with gadgetry or secrecy— it's learning how to find a pattern and explain it in as few words as possible. Before I could legally drink a beer, I was sitting in Langley, writing for the National Intelligence Daily. My audience? The nation's top leaders in developments related to weapons of mass destruction. That experience opened my eyes to the power of being able to aggregate disparate information, link patterns, and communicate all that to decision makers. My time at the CIA significantly shaped my thinking about how much information there is in the world to understand and how difficult it is to find people, systems, and processes to help understand it quickly.

Third, I've learned to identify the good—and bad—of futurist thinking. Futurism has always been a useful tool in my consulting career. And it's an important component of many consulting firms' practices. It is also a personal passion. As a young intern on Capitol Hill, I studied the work of Alvin and Heidi Toffler on the future of warfare and built it into my own research projects. I have been hooked ever since, weaving the best work of futurists into my own thinking. Sometimes, futurists are dead wrong, but they're always interesting and often can help executives make far better strategic decisions. In this book, I use the lessons that I've learned about futurist thinking. I apply those lessons to consulting and make a few predictions about what the future will bring—and how those predictions are relevant to you.

The one guarantee I can make: some of those predictions will be wrong. In fact, being wrong is one of my best qualities. In the spirit of innovation, I believe that the constant practice of making predictions, even when wrong, puts us in a position to leap when other people hedge—to see the iceberg a second before it hits. And that second can make all the difference. So while we may have hits and misses, one thing is certain: having a nimble and innovative mindset is key to survival.

The reason this book took flight: I believe that there is a more cost effective and less complicated way to buy consulting services.

In 2006, I cofounded a firm called Big Sky Associates with a couple of other passionate individuals. Central to the idea of Big Sky is that the consulting profession, even as revenues and profits grew, often failed to give clients the quality and type of advice they needed.

In time, it became clear that the underlying challenge facing our clients wasn't an absence of well-meaning firms out there working hard to do the right thing. There were, and are, many such firms. Like those firms, we put the client first at Big Sky. We hire phenomenal professionals and create a place that is rewarding and fun.

But that isn't enough. We continue to see professional services firms that are doing the right things for their shareholders and clients by extending engagements, broadening their offerings, and growing their workforce. But we continue to watch clients make poor choices and follow bad advice. Further, the very things that make established firms successful for their clients are the things that prevent them from embracing innovation.

Enter Microslices: The future of professional services

This book, *Microslices*, is written to provoke action, and therefore it has to be provocative. The purpose is for the executive buyer to understand the change affecting the consulting firms they hire, what the future holds, and what to do about it. Microslices itself is the inevitable future business model for professional services. **Defined, Microslices is the accelerating specialization, compression, and automation of consulting activities.**

This book is going to walk you into the future.

UNDERSTANDING MICROSLICES

AN OVERVIEW OF MICROSLICES IN PROFESSIONAL SERVICES

The same forces that disrupted industries such as steel and publishing are starting to reshape the consulting industry, with profound implications for its future.

Clayton Christensen

First things first

Are you hoping for a book that is all about big data or Hadoop, the singularity, neuroscience, predictive analytics, artificial intelligence, flying cars, or robot overlords? If so, prepare yourself for profound disappointment.

This book is about the advice business. Period.

That's where we begin and end. In this book, I often refer to the advice business as consulting, mostly because that's my background. Alternatively, I refer to it as "professional services." At your organization, you might call it "contracting" or "advisory services." But most of the ideas in this book are equally applicable to anyone who gives advice for a living.[8]

There are a bevy of fantastic articles, books, TED Talks on YouTube, and online courses that cover big data analytics, neuroscience, nanobots, genetic engineering, and the inevitable singularity in which we will either achieve utopia or lose our jobs. Some of them will be referenced in this book. You absolutely should read them. While we'll hit some high points, this book won't go into the depths of technology trends. We're after something else.

CLAYTON CHRISTENSEN

This book describes the rise of a new business model of consulting referred to in this book as *Microslices*, the factors

8 | I hope this book is a worthy addition to the foundation of great research on professional services by great minds like David Maister and Peter Block. Like their work, this book's ideas and conclusions apply to many professional services, be it law, consulting, accounting, IT services, investment advice, or coaching.

driving its emergence, and the actions you can take now to adapt. It builds on the work first and foremost of the outstanding research of Clayton Christensen, author of *The Innovator's Dilemma*, who predicted the disruption[9] of the consulting industry in a 2013 *Harvard Business Review* article titled "Consulting on the Cusp of Disruption."

Unlike most books about consulting—written for insiders looking to land more clients—this book is written for the *buyer*. You're the executive who wants to understand the rapid change affecting the consulting profession, what the future holds, and how to buy those services both now and over the next 10 to 15 years. If you are a leader in an organization that procures complex and expensive services, this book is for you. If you might get promoted one day and be the guy who has to buy those services, this book is for you.

This book arms you with the information you need to get results from those services faster, cheaper, and better. It gives you real examples that'll increase the return on your fees for any professional service and prepare you for the opportunities and challenges that lie ahead.

/////////////////// A LOOK BACK FROM 2030 ///////////////////

OBSERVATIONS FROM THE FUTURE

I also provide a perspective from the future. I provide anecdotes, warnings, descriptions, and stock picks from 2030.

///

9 | The phenomenon by which an innovation transforms an existing market or sector by introducing simplicity, convenience, accessibility, and affordability where complication and high cost are the status quo.

What Are Microslices, Anyway?

Every consulting project consists of a series of tasks and activities. Back when I started consulting in the 1990s, we seemed to have a lot of five-phase projects. I think they were in five phases because they had to fit neatly on a PowerPoint slide, and six chevrons on a PowerPoint slide changed the mood from "organized" to "menacing." It was a very '90s kind of thing, but that's what we did. I'd bet you've seen something like the graphic below:

On those pre-millennium slides, as a consulting project was subdivided into its constituent activities, chevrons broke down into stages, stages broke down into steps, and steps broke down further into tasks and mini-tasks. You may remember this yourself; it was cutting edge back then. Regardless of what these subcomponents were called, the point is that projects have always broken down as activities into very small pieces. In one firm, we called these activities "kernels," and "slices" has also been used to describe the discrete tasks on a consulting project.

At KPMG, for example, we had a master (or should I say, "monster") PowerPoint file that provided a clickable map of what must have been 150 distinct projects that could occur in different phases of a particular type of engagement. And you could configure those projects as pieces in any number of ways for an engagement, like extremely expensive Legos. This idea of "chunking" a professional services project is not a new one, but new things are happening—and happening rapidly—that make looking at this process with a fresh eye and a fresh approach important. That's where Microslicing comes in.

Microslices are different from our tool at KPMG because they're much smaller and are delivered much faster; as technology and networks of delivery improve, they will become so specialized, automated, and rapidly delivered that they'll deliver value instantly, often with no human intervention. They can then be configured into infinite patterns of any business problem.

There are several trends, which I'll describe in chapters 2–4, which explain why *Microslices* is a better term for what is happening and what that means, but let's get a definition on the table:

Microslices
\m ī (,)kr ō\sl ī\s ēz

The accelerating *specialization*, *compression*, and *automation* of consulting activities. Fully realized it will be the dominant business model of professional services.

Let's break that down a little bit.

Accelerating Specialization

Adam Smith called specialization the "division of labor."[10] Peter Drucker wrote extensively on specialization for knowledge workers.[11] Specialization is not a new idea. Specialization in services is, however, accelerating.

Thomas Malone, author of *The Future of Work*, wrote in *Harvard Business Review* that "thanks to the rise of knowledge work and communications technology, this subdivision of labor has advanced to a point where the next difference in degree will constitute a difference in kind. We are entering an era of hyperspecialization—a very different, and not yet widely understood, world of work."[12]

///////////////////////// A LOOK BACK FROM 2030 /////////////////////////

THE NEED FOR SPEED

In the Microslices model, specialization is so extreme that thousands deliver the work products that we used to deliver with a team of five. The funny thing is, executives don't really even think about "consulting projects" anymore. They have questions and expect answers; they have problems, and they get solutions. By 2025 the typical complex "project," especially for transactional/recommendation work, took only 1/100th of the time required to do the same work in 2020.

///

10 | Adam Smith, *An Inquiry into the Nature and Causes of the Wealth of Nations: A Selected Edition*, ed. Kathryn Sutherland. Oxford: Oxford Paperbacks, 2008.

11 | Peter F. Drucker, "The Coming of the New Organization," *Harvard Business Review*, Jan. 1988.

12 | Thomas W. Malone, Robert Laubacher, and Tammy Johns, "The Big Idea: The Age of Hyperspecialization," *Harvard Business Review*, July–August 2011, https://hbr.org/2011/07/the-big-idea-the-age-of-hyperspecialization/

Accelerating Compression

The second piece of the definition of *Microslices* is the shrinking time it takes to deliver a consulting activity. I don't just mean work is done faster; the *rate* at which projects are *getting faster* is also accelerating. Accelerating compression has profound implications not just for consulting but for knowledge work in general. You already don't have the patience to wait for weeks for interview results from your consulting projects, and those expectations will march relentlessly forward.

Accelerating Automation

"Accelerating automation" is the big thing that changes everything and introduces excitement and pace to this phenomenon. Automation is a key ingredient that enables both hyperspecialization and speed. As you may know, this is already happening in consulting, law, finance, and even medicine.

Even in my own small firm, large parts of our sales and business development processes are automated. We've developed tools internally and partner with other firms to complete tasks in mere hours that, when I started consulting in the 1990s, would've taken weeks.

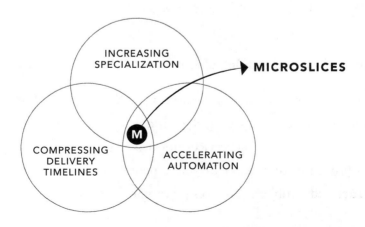

The process of conducting client interviews is a good example of that. At Big Sky Associates, we've developed tools in partnership with other firms to partially automate the process of collecting and aggregating client interview information. Even 30 meetings can take weeks to schedule and organize. Tools available now can automate much of that process and give you nearly the same quality. (When you're talking about cutting the timeline from weeks to a few days, getting close is just fine.)

In short, the range and complexity of consulting activities that can be completed by machines is breathtaking and shows no signs of abating.

/////////////////// A LOOK BACK FROM 2030 ///////////////////

AUTOMAGIC

It's hard to even describe how professional services works in 2030, because to the buyer the process seems seamless, almost like magic. To be sure, it's incredibly complex on the back end. Today machines can access and analyze more information in an hour than existed on earth in 2015. Sometimes the machines are even funny and creative in their solutions, identifying opportunities for disruption themselves.

//

More Than Just a Framework: A New Economic Model

Today there are many minor variations on the consulting business engine, but for the most part, the basic process hasn't changed. If you're buying consulting services, most of the time you're paying an hourly rate for a team of smart people to solve a relatively unstructured problem. Not only are you likely paying a lot of money for those services, your relationship with the consultants is based on your trust in their judgment.

The future, however, is going to be quite different. Microslices differs from the traditional model of consulting in a number of fundamental ways.

In the old model, pricing is primarily hourly. In the new model, pricing is fixed or value based. In the old model, time and expenses are the basis of pricing of an engagement. If it took you eight weeks to do the project, you were going to get paid for eight weeks of work. In the new model, pricing is completely independent from how long something takes. Whether it takes a day or a year, value is value.

The old model really is a pure service: a custom activity performed for a fee. In the new model, productization—prepackaged solutions, already a key component of most large firms' strategies—dominates. Even at top firms like McKinsey & Company, Boston Consulting Group, and Bain & Company, solutions that solve discrete problems are packaged for clients.

The old model of consulting also features broad diversity and integration of services under one roof. One firm assembles a team of its own employees to deliver that solution, which would include everything from preliminary research to change management to quantitative modeling to graphic design right through installing software and hardware. Occasionally they use partners, but for the most part one firm drives the bus.

In the new model, rapidly assembled teams of niche players solve a problem, some of whom may not be aware or a part of the overall project objective. They're just going to attack it in their specialized, tiny slice: their Microslice. As a buyer, you might be concerned that there won't be "one-stop shop" firms that provide soup-to-nuts services. Fortunately, the trends described in this book enable a "facilitated network"[13] of service providers that make it easy for you to get what you need, even if it's from many firms on one project.

In the old model, firms have high-profile physical spaces in markets like New York and London—and they provide a high-touch environment where clients can come to the office with Persian rugs and commissioned art. It is a high-prestige business with a setting to match. In the new model, placeless delivery becomes the norm. You may not know where the work is performed.

In the old model, teams of people deliver together; there is a premium placed on being physically located with the team or the client. With the rise of trends described in this book, the professional services industry is shifting to a mixed human/machine model, where people, physically dispersed, work with software, their own algorithms, and other humans to solve small parts of a bigger problem. Those teams become less about the dynamic of the physically colocated team and more about the delivery model of how those things get placed at the right time, in the right place.

Finally, and likely the difference between old and new models that is hardest to swallow, is the shift away from what David Maister called "the trusted advisor."[14] In the traditional professional services model, the trusted advisor builds a relationship with the client—to a

---

13 | The "facilitated network" is a concept coined by Clayton Christensen to describe how consulting firms and individuals may band together to more seamlessly deliver services.

14 | David Maister, Charles H. Green, and Robert Galford, *The Trusted Advisor*. Knopf, 2012.

large extent, that trust of professionalism and expertise is the basis by which consultants grow their businesses and why clients hire them. The trusted advisor model, while still important, is slowly giving way to one where price, terms, schedule, and purchase are far more driven by the expected value of the result.

I've provided a quick overview of Microslices and what the concept means for the future of professional services. However, you should remember that while Microslices will become dominant over time, it is already happening. In chapter 9, I present several case studies of companies that demonstrate the Microslicing model today, in 2015. You'll read about:

- A company that started out as a traditional advertising firm and transformed itself into an automated personal branding engine that delivers thousands of analyses a day.

- A start-up that's replacing traditional new hire coaching and consulting with a brilliant toolkit for managers of governments and Fortune 500 executives.

- A consulting automation toolkit that can take hundreds of hours of work and reduce it to minutes, saving their clients millions.

- An advanced analytics company that partners with consulting firms, government agencies, and other knowledge workers to "read" hundreds of thousands of pages of unstructured information and make sense of it.

Enough introduction. In the next three chapters we'll take a look at the three main factors that are driving the Microslices phenomenon and explore how each impacts consulting and, most importantly, your business.

CHAPTER 1 SUMMARY

○ Microslices is a book about consulting but applies to just about any kind of advice-giving business. If you hire consultants, coaches, lawyers, accountants, or anyone who charges a fee for professional help or expertise, you might find this book useful.

○ Unlike most books about consulting, this book is for the executive buyer of consulting services (but should be useful for practitioners).

○ Specifically, it addresses the rise of a new business and economic model for management consulting, called Microslices.

○ Microslices is defined as the accelerating compression, specialization, and automation of consulting or similar advice-giving activities. Many activities will become faster and hyperspecialized, performed without human intervention.

○ Consulting hasn't changed much in the last 100 years; it is (mostly) still based on hourly fees, broadly defined services, large integrated "do it all" firms, and high-profile, high-touch physical presence.

○ That model is giving way to one in which networked delivery models, value or fixed fees, productized offerings, hyperspecialized niche players, and distributed teams of teams are the norm.

○ Part I of this book is about the three drivers of the disruptive innovation driving the emergence of Microslices, and part II tells you what to do about it.

DRIVING FORCES— DATA SCIENCE

You can have data without information, but you cannot have information without data.

–Daniel Keys Moran

ate Silver. Larry Page. Peter Thiel. Jeff Hammerbacher. Peter Norvig. Some of these guys would have been unknowns 30 years ago, maybe even 15 years ago—the nerds that ski instructors would beat up in between Duran Duran shows in an '80s movie.

Now they're like movie stars. The common gift of these data scientists: they all share an extraordinary ability to work magic with increasingly massive data sets. Nate Silver started out working in sabermetrics and is now famous for his election predictions. Larry Page cofounded Google to "organize the world's information." Peter Thiel cofounded PayPal and Palantir. These aren't just good businessmen; they are changing the world by making better use of data. And unlike the heroes of 20th century business, they're doing it with a wardrobe that's 10 percent suit and tie and 90 percent hoodie.

Data scientists aren't new, but they are newly important. With the advent of big data, the lowly statistician has been transformed from hobbyist to master of the most complex problems humanity has ever conceived. That last part may sound dramatic, but it's true. What this chapter is going to explore is how it's changing the consulting delivery model.

//////////////////// A LOOK BACK FROM 2030 ////////////////////

BUZZWORDS OF THE FUTURE

It's pretty funny to look back from 2030 and read about "data science" and "big data" and "big data analytics." What you call "data science" we call "employment." You're going to reflect on these buzzwords in a few years and wince. All these things are just work in 2030. That's just what people (and machines) do.

//

When I was a kid, the heroes of our generation in the frontier of science were astronauts at NASA. Unfortunately, nobody really talks about those heroes anymore (although they are still most certainly heroic). Most people under 30, if asked to name an astronaut, might think first of Lisa Nowak, the mission specialist who drove across the country in a space diaper that she allegedly stole from a NASA mission supply locker.[15]

---

15 | As crazy as it sounds, this is a true story, although in court proceedings Nowak denied using the space diapers. She was nonetheless discharged from the Navy under less than honorable conditions. Source: "Lisa Nowak," Wikipedia.

HEROES

JOHN GLENN   STEVE JOBS   NATE SILVER   PETER THIEL

THEN   NOW

I don't mean to disparage NASA. Not only are they a former client of mine, they're doing some of the most amazing work imaginable, not only in matters related to space but also in a lot of the trends that we talk about in this book. I'm simply observing that the public's perception of what constitutes "cool" science has changed.

One of the biggest challenges of technology trends and their acceleration is the sheer volume of data that is produced.

YEAR		SOURCE
1900		TYPEWRITERS • PRINTING PRESS HANDWRITTEN LETTERS RADIO • TELEGRAPH
1950		TELEVISION
1980		EARLY COMPUTING PUBLIC ACCESS TO VIDEO
2000		SMALL SENSORS MOBILE
TODAY		24-HOUR VIDEO • WEARABLES SATELLITE/DRONE IMAGERY CONTINUOUS WEB AND MOBILE DEV

Looking at the chart, we see sources of data categorized by decades. For example, in 1900, data was produced by typewriters and the printing press, handwritten letters, and, in limited cases, radio and telegraph. In 1950 it shifted to television. In 1980 it shifted further to early computing and public access to video and shifted further again in 2000 with widespread adoption of small sensors and mobile. Today, data sources are too voluminous to list: continuous, 24-hour video in millions of locations, wearables, satellite and drone imagery, and continuous web and mobile development.

For example, a single machine writes approximately 40,000 Wikipedia entries a day. Computers create content themselves—and a lot of it.

Information Overload

When I was hired at the CIA in the mid-1990s, I was absolutely floored by the amount of information at my fingertips, and I was coming from a university that had great library resources. I couldn't understand how the CIA could manage all that data.

Part of my job was to try to cull through a lot of it and make conclusions. The CIA employed statisticians, but they were often working on more obscure data sets, often related to economics. The statisticians didn't permeate the organization, and statistical literacy wasn't necessarily a cultural norm, although I suspect that is changing.

Around that same time—in 1997, which is about the same time I was at the CIA—Michael Lesk wrote a paper titled "How Much Information Is There in the World?"[16] In that paper, he

16 | Michael Lesk. "How Much Information Is There in the World?" Retrieved Apr. 20, 2015, http://www.lesk.com/mlesk/ksg97/ksg.html.

estimated that the total "professional information" in the world totaled about 12,000 petabytes. (To be clear, that was the total data *in existence in the world*. Not just the data created that year but the total in existence.) Today, IBM claims that we *create* 2.5 quintillion bytes, which is about 2,200 petabytes of data per day.

That means in an average 2014 or 2015 week, we create more data than existed in the history of the world in 1997.

If you've read much about "big data," you know that the volume of data created over time is an *exponential* curve (or a straight line on a logarithmic scale). According to research by companies like EMC and IBM, 90 percent of the world's data has been created *in the last 24 months*. In the amount of time that elapsed from the time I started this book and when you're reading it, data volume has at least doubled.

Data Volume before the Acceleration of Data Science: An Insurmountable Obstacle

Before the adoption of data science began to accelerate, volume was a huge problem. When I was consulting for both Fortune 500 companies and the intelligence agencies, the pace of data creation was far outpacing our ability to analyze it. In the 1990s and 2000s, the problem was so new and seemingly complicated that there was a lot of confusion about its nature and whether it would continue unabated. In many fields, the initial response was to try to find ways to limit collection of data or to be more selective in collection, to ease the burden on analysis. Unfortunately, that doesn't work too well when sensors of all types are getting cheaper and smaller. That's like trying to fight a flood by using better buckets. Water's still comin'.

The only possible solution to the huge data problem was to reinvigorate the profession of statistics and expand it to people who could not just run the stats but could also identify, interpret, analyze, and otherwise make sense and tell stories with vast quantities of data. And not just vast quantities of data but a wide variety of data.

Big Data
\ˈbig\ \ˈdā-tə

Data sets, typically consisting of billions or trillions of records, that are so vast and complex that they require new and powerful computational resources to process.

Within data science, the sexier cousin of statistics, a variety of skills and competencies manifest themselves in diverse ways. While some might dismiss data science as just a new word for statistics, data science is in fact more multifaceted and brings together skills not just in math and statistics but also in creative inquiry, graphic design, and programming. This new mix of skills enables a new kind of consultant to rapidly organize and analyze massive volumes of information, previously lost in interview notes, proprietary BI databases, simulation software, or any number of informational black holes.

Even when dealing with unstructured data, we can now ask questions we couldn't ask before on data sets that we didn't know we had—or we thought were useless. Data science helps us reorganize data in a way that becomes meaningful. It changes the way we think about our own organizations. It also changes the way our advisors organize and interpret data.

Despite the lure of technology and the promise of big data, the real "secret sauce" of data science is the application of creative analytical techniques that propose incisive hypotheses and creative conclusions from that data. In short, it's not really the tech that's sexy; it's the creative interpretation of evidence and data.

Collecting lots of data is mostly useless without the ability to design techniques, predictive analytics, machine learning tools, and visualization techniques that provide insight into what it means.

I see this every day in my firm's work on security, employee suitability, and insider threats. Big Sky often helps large organizations protect themselves from internal threats—like information theft, sabotage, and even workplace violence. Data science is transforming our clients' ability to deter, detect, and mitigate these threats by providing a means to sift through mountains of consensually provided employee data as well as network activity monitoring and physical security systems.

The main downside our clients face: there can be false positives in data-driven behavioral analysis. However, the overwhelming benefits far outweigh the risks. Granted, if you have a huge work force, and each employee can contribute a large amount of data, you can't possibly hope to detect things that you would know on an interpersonal level. Data science does, though, allow large organizations to screen a select group of people who pose higher risk, and focus attention and intervention on those people.

If you work for a bank, or if you're in the critical infrastructure business like an energy company or an aerospace company, or certainly government agencies, the damage that one person can do is pretty catastrophic if you don't catch them in time.

This same concept applies to the people who might steal secrets from Boeing and give them to Airbus. It applies to an energy company who might be concerned that there's an employee who has a vendetta against nuclear power and might try to set off a bomb and damage a nuclear reactor. While data science may not give us the ability to prevent all bad things from happening, it does give us a better shot at identifying, prioritizing, and limiting security risks.

While technology gets all the press, the data science behind the technology is where the magic often happens. Data science gives us an opportunity to identify patterns that might not have been apparent using simple statistics, anecdotal evidence, or intuition. Applied machine learning, a growing segment of the data science profession, holds the promise of systems and algorithms that automatically retrain themselves based on results. Google's DeepMind project recently released an algorithm that teaches itself how to play old Atari video games—a transformational breakthrough for 1980s schoolchildren worldwide. The programmers didn't tell it how to play or even what the rules are—it learns from the ground up (kind of like a human would).[17]

You already engage these kinds of algorithms on a daily basis. The simplest examples of this would be something like Netflix's recommendation engine and LinkedIn's "who else you may know" tool. Those are still in the beginning stages—Netflix may be able to accurately predict what I like in a general sort of way, but it doesn't know what kind of mood I'm in at any given moment.

17 | Rebecca Jacobson. "Artificial intelligence program teaches itself to play Atari games—and it can beat your high score." February 25, 2015, http://www.pbs.org/newshour/rundown/artificial-intelligence-program-teaches-play-atari-games-can-beat-high-score/

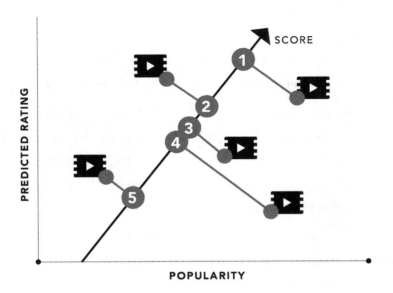

SCORE

PREDICTED RATING

POPULARITY

NETFLIX RECOMMENDATIONS: BEYOND THE 5 STARS, BY XAVIER AMATRIAIN AND JUSTIN BASILICO
(PERSONALIZATION SCIENCE AND ENGINEERING), 2012.

In Netflix's case, there is a diminishing return over time on prediction efficiency. Every time they run one of their competitions to improve their prediction model, they get a smaller marginal result. That's not because they're not trying, it's because we haven't yet solved some fundamental problems about the limits of AI, predictive analytics, and machine learning. When we have a better relationship, better *communication* directly between humans and machines, those predictive analytics models will dramatically improve.

Hopefully, you're now sold on the importance of data science, but to really understand it one must understand what data science is *not*.

Data Science Is Not...

Let me be really clear:

Data science and technology are not the same thing. Technology enables advanced data science, but data science is not hardware. In some cases, data science is enabled by software, but data science will not be performed by the IT guy in your company.

If technology is best represented by Bill Gates or Larry Ellison, "data science" is personified by Nate Silver, the American statistician and writer who uses predictive analytics to analyze baseball and elections. Data scientists are not another flavor of computer scientist or technology consultant.

To look at it in another light, imagine this: the IT guy is kind of like a traditional publisher. The publisher buys the paper, prints the books, binds them, and then distributes the books. They provide the vector and possibly some of the tools to get the author's ideas to the market. But it's the author who gives the book meaning. Without the data scientists, technology would just be the equivalent of paper and glue and delivery trucks and a Kindle.

What Data Science Is...

Data science is a complex, multifaceted discipline. Perhaps the best breakdown I've read was written by Vincent Granville of Analytic Bridge. He explains the overlaps and distinctions among a wide variety of analytical skill sets and techniques related to data science. While you'd really have to study the nuances he presents to create a definition, the figure on the opposite page, drawn by Granville himself, does a nice job of showing the complex interaction of skills involved in contemporary data science.[18]

18 | Vincent Granville. "Building blocks of data science." February 27, 2015. http://www.datasciencecentral.com/profiles/blogs/ building-blocks-of-data-science?xg_source=activity

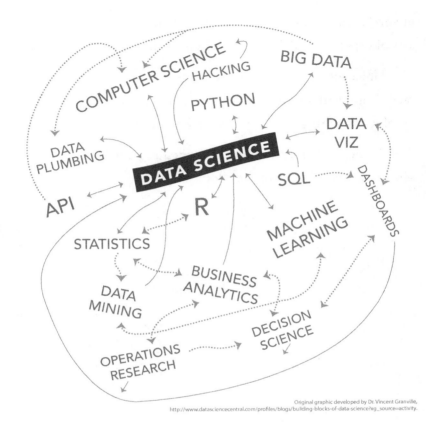

Original graphic developed by Dr. Vincent Granville,
http://www.datasciencecentral.com/profiles/blogs/building-blocks-of-data-science/xg_source=activity.

Data science is just as concerned with *masterful inquiry* as it is with *technical mastery*. The art of asking incredible questions, testing hypotheses, validating results, and using the scientific method is at the heart of data science. Sometimes that means getting results you don't like. Data science is first and foremost about asking the right questions and discerning patterns that yield the best answer for the problem you're trying to solve.

Data science is the discipline that blends math and statistics, computer science, creativity, business expertise, and fairy dust. It's this "special sauce" that represents data science's multidisciplinary arsenal of skills, which is nearly impossible to find in one person. These "unicorns" who master the full range of these skills are exceedingly rare. It often takes a team of folks with multiple sets of expertise to deliver the desired result.

Unicorns aside, one of the biggest challenges data science faces is a talent shortage. Consulting firms, and companies that employ consulting firms, are starving for science skills.

To be sure, the number of students graduating with data science or related degrees is exploding.

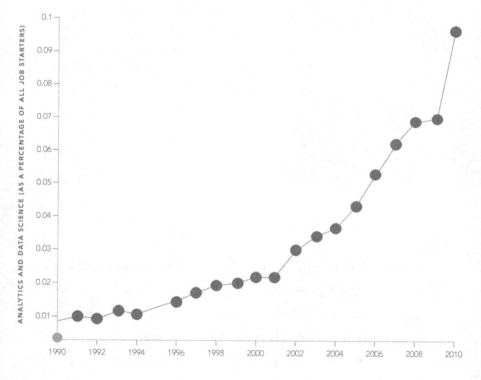

GRAPH ADAPTED FROM RADAR.OREILLY.COM ARTICLE "BUILDING DATA SCIENCE TEAMS." BY DJ PATIL.

But that aside, the biggest obstacle to Microslices is the ability to cultivate and deploy enough talent with the right skills to solve the problems that consulting and other professional services firms are facing.

The variety of problems that a data scientist can now solve with the right tools is amazing. For example: they can score your workforce to predict success or failure in a job. They can help you pick top acquisition targets for your company. They can advise you on the probability that a division or a location of your company will underperform. They can help you pick a better bottle of wine by aggregating data about weather and rainfall in the south of France. They can tell stories using visualization that make complex information accessible and actionable by the nontechnical reader. They can help save lives by reducing medical errors or identifying patterns of risk for workplace violence.

But can data science evolve without presenting threats to individual liberty and privacy? Respected computer scientist and writer Jaron Lanier,[19] in his book on the possible effects of strong AI, expresses skepticism—bordering on alarm—that governments and the economy can adapt. His concerns and those like them are legitimate, but I am more optimistic. Market economies have demonstrated healthy resilience to disruptive innovation by creating entirely new classes of jobs and professions that deal with new kinds of problems and solutions. As we understand the risks presented by emerging trends, demand will increase for ever more rigorous protections. Those protections may take the form of laws, but equally important will be the market demand for privacy-enhancing technology that is easy to use.

---

19 | Jaron Lanier. *Who Owns the Future?* New York: Simon & Schuster, 2013.

A SOCIETY BUILT FROM DATA

Here in 2030, data science so permeates the thinking, organization, and systems of every company and organization on earth that it not only solves problems we've identified, but smart data scientists have designed algorithms that help identify the problems that need to be solved in the first place. Enabled by AI and machine learning, this has displaced even the analytical and diagnostic role of the consultant—companies have a much better understanding of their own problems and opportunities. Consultants focus instead on arranging networks of specialist AIs and other service providers and on assisting executives in making final choices among the new opportunities presented to them.

Every organization should be scrambling to learn about data science and find ways to employ it as soon as possible. At a minimum, as an executive buyer of advisory services, it's imperative that you select partners and consultants that not only want to sell you analytics solutions but also weave data science into their day-to-day thinking about nontechnical problems. In short, data science is a mindset, not a tool.

What Data Science Means for Professional Services and Microslices

If you're an executive in a large organization, you're aware that data is proliferating and that you need data science in order to do something about it. The question is, what role does data science play?

First, data science facilitates faster delivery of professional services. With more sophisticated methods applied to both big data sets and smaller data sets, data science becomes more accessible to nonquantitative organizations. So even if you're an organization that doesn't really consider itself quantitative, there's a good chance that data science is going to find a way to make your people, strategy, and execution better.

Second, data science allows deeper specialization of professional service providers. As the complexity and volume of information available in functions and subfunctions increases, data science will facilitate more complex analysis on narrower topics. Instead of analyzing the onboarding process in aggregate, for example, your advisors may specialize in the initial manager meetings. This is a trend that occurs naturally in consulting, but when data scientists are armed with tools that allow them to focus on narrower problems and larger data sets, hyperspecialization will become the rule.

Finally, data science is going to provide the basis for the automation of consulting tasks. As I mentioned earlier in this chapter, AI and machine learning are typically associated with technology but in reality are driven by data science. This crucial development will help consulting firms focus only on those activities that require humans, leaving "brute force" analysis, data collection, and even some recommendations to algorithms.

This third effect of data science on professional services is certain to meet resistance—not only from the professionals who may be displaced but also by our knowledge worker culture. As you know, cultural resistance to technology is not new. As Malcolm Gladwell adeptly explains in *The Tipping Point*, change can be gradual—until it isn't.

One idea central to Microslices, and which I'll explain in more depth in part II, is the network delivery model, in which many hyperspecialized professional services firms rapidly assemble distributed teams to solve a client problem. Without data science, that model is limited to those networks of providers who can identify each other, broker agreements and partnerships, and coordinate delivery. However, data science can help manage and optimize that networked delivery model.

> *"...in the early 1980s, a big part of [the consultant's] job was assembling data on the market and competitors. Today that work is of¬ten outsourced to market research companies such as Gartner and Forrester, to facilitated networks that link users with industry experts such as Gerson Lehrman Group (GLG), and to database providers such as IMS Health."[20]*

What happens when the aforementioned companies assemble a facilitated network? Can they assemble and analyze that data with quickly produced algorithms using data science? As data becomes available via open APIs (see the next chapter) the networked delivery model becomes enabled by data science—it facilitates cross-organizational and cross-provider analytical work in a way that is currently difficult and time consuming.

Taking that a step further, can data science help you choose what kind of analysis you need in the first place? This network of human specialists is a real trend that's already happening. But we're in an in-between phase. Soon, data science will be able to

20 | Clayton M. Christensen, Dina Wang, and Derek van Bever, "Consulting on the Cusp of Disruption," *Harvard Business Review,* October 2013.

rapidly assemble, analyze, and interpret data from within your company—and *outside* of your company—to come up with a completely new solution that doesn't resemble a consulting engagement designed today.

Data science affects all kinds of professional services—not just data science related consulting, big data consulting, or IT consulting. If you provide advice for a living, there will be no such thing as "soft" consulting anymore. Even the leadership coaches out there, who will give motivational speeches to your firm, can, will, and must be enhanced by the application of data science.

Again, that will happen gradually, and some of those disciplines in consulting can certainly lag behind others. But what companies will quickly realize is this: the application of data science, the ability to mine information about what's successful, and the use of the scientific method to determine what works and what doesn't will not just apply to technical disciplines but to nontechnical disciplines.

As an executive, you have to lead the charge for data, even if you don't have the expertise. You should demand data science from your trusted advisors, and we'll talk about how to go about that later. Consultants are going to have to adapt to how data science replaces many of their traditional functions, from data collection to analysis to prediction to recommendations.

The funny thing is that consultants do some of the best writing on data science that I've read. I have found that some of the best sources of great insight about data science come right from the big consulting firms—McKinsey, Deloitte, Accenture, IBM. However, many of these firms do not apply that insight to their own business model; they do not evaluate how they can use what they're recommending to clients inside their own organizations.

Why? Because large, competitive organizations may understand an important trend, but because they are so dependent on a particular kind of business model, they are unable—or unwilling—to shift to a new way of working. Professional services executives, like executives in previously disrupted industries, make claims that they are "different," that their model is based on trust, or that their hundred-year-old brand is impregnable. In law, consulting, accounting, and similar businesses that have traditionally been dominated by brand and reputation, executives may claim that too many functions could never be commoditized. They are wrong.

There are a handful of consulting firms (and law firms, and accounting firms) that are aware of what's happening and are actively taking steps to adapt. The trick for you is to know which one you're hiring.

Based on everything that we've discussed in this chapter, imagine the value you might be overlooking, not just in the data you're collecting but in all the information that passes through your doors that you're not even aware of. Data is not just what you capture, it's everything that's potentially captured. And if someone isn't there who can interpret it, it just passes you by. Many executives read this as an imperative to invest in big data technology. However, I argue that it's imperative to invest in data science literacy in both your workforce and your advisors.

ORGANIZATIONAL DEVELOPMENT GETS MICROSLICED

In the 2020s, many firms stuck with their longstanding HR consultants, whom they trusted implicitly. But one challenge that proved intractable was how to encourage healthy behavior in the workforce. They tried every tried-and-true change management method: strategy sessions, scorecards, paying for people to get gym memberships, and even health contests. They brought in health advisors and nutritionists, exercise physiologists—anything they could possibly do to try to help their workforce be healthy and more productive. [21]

Then, in about 2022 a five-person start-up came along that developed an algorithm that (on an opt-in basis) identified high-health-risk employees based on hundreds of data points collected on thousands of employees nearly continuously. Not only did sick leave drop by 20 percent for adopters, the algorithm detected ten employees' impending heart attack six hours before it would've otherwise occurred. That little data-driven consulting firm, and its Microslice that focused on this very narrow problem that enabled a data science application, saved lives and saved the company money. And as you might expect, many longtime HR consultants' contracts quietly ended.

Imagine being able to compile, interpret, and communicate the data that could be captured just at the threshold of your building's front door. Cameras on the property could detect arrival patterns, who comes late, who looks tired, who looks rushed, who

21 | Aviva Rutkin. "Machine predicts heart attack 4 hours before doctors." *New Scientist*, August 2014. Issue 2981.

interacts cheerfully with their coworkers, or who opens the door for others. Your advisors could help you tie your organizational processes and goals to the mining and interpretation of that data in near real time. They'd be able to tell you the moment someone should take a break, and that employee might get a prompt on his or her screen telling them to take a rest based on how often they're getting coffee or how often they're clicking on social media. They could flag employees who are performing jobs unsuitable to their current condition and help reallocate them to other tasks where they could be more effective (and happier).

Now imagine what your advisors and consultants could do with all that information and how it would benefit your organizational purpose, employee output, morale, and, in the end, the mark you can make on the world as an organization. Is this desirable or even ethical? I believe that what seems outlandish to us now will be viewed very differently in ten years. Put to the right use, information, when understood and put into action, is business altering, life altering, and society altering. Many executives currently use consultants to make these kinds of changes, so their ability to leverage data science is crucial to your success.

CHAPTER 2 SUMMARY

○ Data science has become among the most fascinating and admired disciplines in the world.

○ Data science's rise is directly correlated with the explosion of information and the massive challenge of interpreting it.

○ While related to statistics and technology, data science is much more. Its value is in the "special sauce" that connects a variety of disciplines.

○ There is confusion around the term "data science." Does it mean statistics? Technology? It is both—and neither.

○ Data science allows for the creative application of information, largely because it is, among other things, the interplay of math, technology, visualization, and computer science.

○ Data science is the first critical enabler of Microslices, allowing consultants to work faster, specialize deeply, and automate many functions.

○ Data science literacy is crucial for executives who purchase consulting services, because data science enables professional services firms to solve new kinds of problems in new ways.

○ To unlock the value in your organization, investing in data science is even more important than investing in technology.

CHAPTER 3

DRIVING FORCES— KEY TECHNOLOGIES

I believe computing will evolve faster in the next 10 years than it ever has before . . . We are nearing the point where computers and robots will be able to see, move, and interact naturally, unlocking many new applications and empowering people even more.

—Bill Gates, 40th Anniversary Letter to Microsoft, April 2015

n light of the title of this chapter, I'd like to remind the reader that this is *not* a book about technology. It's a book about how organizations buy advice. Nonetheless, we have to cover this topic in *Microslices*. Because regardless of how much trepidation I have about technology predictions, it is a crucial enabler of the new professional services firm.

Key Techs driving microslices

Big data, computing power, and open APIs are important, but they are only three gears in a complex and mutually reinforcing set of technologies that will enable Microslices.

- natural user interfaces
- natural language processing
- display technologies
- sensor proliferation
- stronger AI
- machine learning
- human-machine interfaces

The idea that technology is becoming a transformative force in service delivery might seem obvious, but it wasn't years ago. David Maister, whose work on professional services has been revered for years, barely acknowledged it in *Managing the Professional Service Firm* (2003, rev. 2007), which I kept on my desk like a Bible when I was a midlevel consultant. That great book, at 384 pages long, features the word "technology" only *11 times*.

That aside, Maister made a crucial point about automation.

While most firms recognize [the opportunity to automate basic processes], few have fully exploited the opportunities to tap into the power of the microcomputer. In large part, this lag is due to the entrenched practice of charging clients by the hour for work done by professional staff. This cir-

cumstance has inhibited the large-scale adoption of tools that substitute machines for person-hours.

When I reread that passage recently, I nearly fell out of my chair. Here we have David Maister asking, "Why don't consulting firms use more automation to deliver?" That was *22 years ago.*

The answer is simple: *Because it's not in their interest.* It is often more lucrative to charge by the hour—especially if there are overruns. In addition, automation can cut down on billable hours. Automation should benefit you, the buyer, but few firms peddle their services based on value instead of hours.

We're going to come back to this idea of what will make the new firm successful in part II of this book, so file that idea away for later.

Stay with Me, Even If You're Not a Geek

If you don't work with technology, you may feel an urge to jump ahead to the next chapter. Hang in there with me. Having even a basic understanding of the topic is absolutely critical to your ability to choose the right advisory firm, and you cannot delegate it to someone else. Don't be that guy who has his assistant print out all of his emails.

Consulting and Technology: Longtime Partners in Crime

Since its infancy, consulting has walked hand in hand with technology development. Every major technological advance since the 1920s and 1930s—mainframe computing, the microcomputer, client server, networking, the Internet, social media, nanotech, and big data—every single one of these developments has increased consulting revenue. As new technology emerges, consulting firms develop new skills and deploy that expertise to their customers.

INNOVATION BOOSTS NICHE PLAYERS

This chart looks very different in 2030. Microslices have driven so much specialization and innovation by niche players that "big firm" consulting growth stalled out around 2018. Niche players all over the world—individuals, small firms, and application developers—displaced the big guys. That said, several of the large players who saw Microslices coming adapted their business model and have seen tremendous growth in automated products and services.

///

TECH

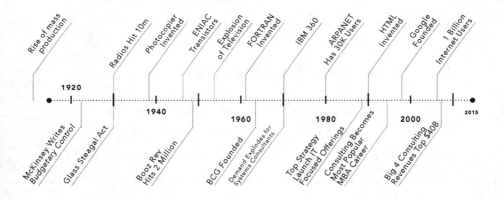

CONSULTING

Good consultants are always reading. They introduce their clients to the newest ideas, which is one of the best roles they can play. For those of us in the consulting profession, it's also one of our favorite parts of the job. We are paid to learn and share that learning with others. It is a wonderful arrangement for both parties.

Many executives do not have the time to run an organization, focus on their strengths, and stay on top of all those technology trends. It's just not doable, and that's the reason consultants are a reasonable expense for many organizations.

I expect that most readers of this book are pretty up to speed—if not from their own study then from their advisors—on concepts like big data, the Internet of Things, Moore's Law,[22] the mobile economy, and any number of other terms that capture the tech zeitgeist. Growth in professional services has been enhanced by companies' and governments' need for advice on how to choose and implement technology.

Even in my own small firm, projects that don't start out as technology projects end up as technology projects. I've advised national security clients on how to improve the speed and quality of processes. But those processes almost always need technology to fully scale, for example, from 100 tasks a month to 100,000 tasks a month. At Big Sky, we helped one client cut 20 percent from a portfolio company's operating costs, but those cuts meant changing technology. Even law firms (longtime holdouts) have no choice but to be tech savvy. This is a big reason why even "pure" strategy firms of the 1960s and 1970s evolved more and more into technology firms, even to the point of being intimately involved in implementation.

Technology walks hand in hand with consulting. But do professional services firms drink their own Kool-Aid and use tech to improve the services they deliver to you? Not always.

---

22 | Most people have come to understand Moore's Law as the doubling of computing power every two years. That's not entirely accurate. Moore's Law in fact predicted that the number of transistors placed on a single chip doubles every two years (which has held up so far). However, the law has become a useful shorthand in referring to the generally accelerating technology progress in many fields, including computer science, biotech, robotics, and nanotechnology.

The Best Firms Practice What They Preach

Selling advice about technology and adopting it as a tool you also use aren't the same thing.

At one large consulting firm where I once worked, we were trying to build the world's best website for a client. But my employer's own website was one of the world's worst. I've been on teams that admonish clients for not developing and managing internal processes properly, yet have poorly developed and managed internal processes themselves. Similarly, there are top-notch companies that produce world-class research on the technologies I describe in this chapter but fail to apply those technologies to their own service delivery.

That doesn't seem right, because on a fundamental level it *isn't* right. It's the consulting equivalent of having an obese, chain-smoking doctor demand that you lose weight and exercise. Professional services firms should be focusing the lens of technology on themselves to improve delivery. However, which technologies are most important to improving delivery? Further—are those technologies the ones that will not just make incremental improvement but will fundamentally improve the value equation between you and your consultants?

The Three Technologies That Matter Most

The bottom line is that technology will continue to be the driver of consulting change. This book can't cover them all, but there are three developments I think matter most.

As Microslices develop, you'll learn more about the interdependent parts of these technologies and how they enable other technologies and further change. For now, I want you to understand the "three major muscle groups," if you will, of Microslices technology enablers:

- ○ The proliferation and integration of very large data sets (we'll call this "big data," even though I don't want to)

- ○ Processing power and the artificial intelligence it enables

- ○ Application innovation and open APIs

Big Data

"Big data" must be the most annoying buzzword in the history of, well, buzzwords. If Martin Lawrence's signature drag character and the nerdiest hero from *Star Trek: The Next Generation* had a tryst while attending a TED Talk, the baby would be named Big Data. However, because I am a realist about technology trends and how people talk about them, I'm going to use the term anyway. Please accept my apologies. I think NewVantage's CEO Randy Bean got it right when he wrote, "Big data is a term that captures the zeitgeist. Love it or hate it, big data is a term that has caught on."[23]

The fact is that big data and the scale and scope of big data are almost incomprehensible and are incomprehensibly important. This has less to do with the size of data sets in zettabytes and more to do with the layers of innovation and application that can be applied to them. You're the kid, and the data is the candy store.

In *The Second Machine Age: Work, Progress, and Prosperity in a Time of Brilliant Technologies*, Erik Brynjolfsson and Andrew McAfee facetiously predicted that digitization yields so much growth in data that we're going to "run out of metric system." In

23 | Randy Bean, "Big Data Fatigue?" MIT Sloan Management Review, June 23, 2014.

other words, we're generating a hell of a lot of new information and *fast*. This isn't something that's happening in dark corridors in Silicon Valley; you and your company and the people who work for it are the ones generating this data.

The Cisco Global Cloud Index similarly predicts that global cloud IP traffic will hit 5.3 zettabytes a year by 2017.[24] That's 5.3 x 10^{21} bytes—a pretty big exponent. A zettabyte (ZB) is well beyond my ability to visualize, but think about it this way: 1 ZB is 1,000 exabytes (EB), 1 EB is 1,000 petabytes (PB), and 1 PB is 1,000 terabytes (TB). A reasonably sized hard drive in 2015 is 1 TB—so you'd need about five *billion* of them to get to 5.3 zettabytes. EMC, a longtime leader in storage and the manufacturer of some of the largest storage arrays in the world, explained it this way: you'd have to watch the TV series *24* continuously for 125 million years to get a zettabyte's worth of Jack Bauer.

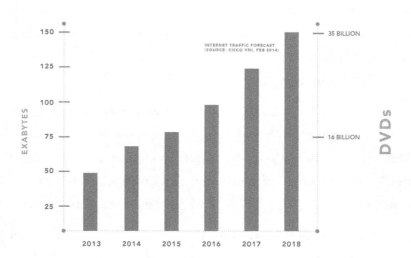

24 | Annual global cloud IP traffic will reach 5.3 zettabytes by the end of 2017. By 2017, global cloud IP traffic will reach 443 exabytes per month (up from 98 exabytes per month in 2012). Global cloud IP traffic will increase nearly 4.5-fold over the next five years. Overall, cloud IP traffic will grow at a CAGR of 35 percent from 2012 to 2017. Global cloud IP traffic will account for more than two-thirds of total data center traffic by 2017.

Companies and governments are making massive investments in big data technologies and the processing power required to deal with it. IDC predicts that from 2015 to 2020, spending on cloud-based big data will outpace spending on on-site solutions by a factor of three.[25] The volume generated by everything that gets measured and stored over that five-year period will make the last five years' data explosion seem like a drop. Not a drop in a bucket—a drop in an ocean.

So what the heck is all this data, and where is it coming from? In 2016, analysts may stop using the phrase "Internet of Things" and start using "Internet of Everything." The variety of sensors we can put on ourselves, the equipment in our companies, our people, our things, our locations, our information, our rooms, our construction projects, and our fleets is going to explode. Sensors will be all over everything and will create more and more data.[26]

Applied to consulting, the growth of available data, the storage available per dollar, and the democratization of access to storage all mean that you and your advisors will have the ability to store, access, and share an exponentially growing body of knowledge related to your specific business problems.

If you want to know what's going on in a room—for example, the cafeteria in your headquarters—you'll have the potential to know

25 | IDC. "IDC Reveals Worldwide Big Data and Analytics Predictions for 2015." December 11, 2014. http://www.idc.com/getdoc.jsp?containerId=prUS25329114

26 | Researchers and futurists alike described this as the "Trillion Sensor Economy" in which 100 billion connected devices, with ten more sensors each, will vastly expand our ability to collect data and interact with each other and with connected devices.

Source: Peter Diamandis. "The World in 2025: 8 Predictions for the Next 10 Years." May 11, 2015. http://singularityhub.com/2015/05/11/the-world-in-2025-8-predictions-for-the-next-10-years/

that there are ten people walking around, each of whom might have four or five sensors on their person. You're going to have climate control data about light, temperature, and ambient noise in the room. You're going to know how hot the water is, how cold the water is. You're going to know how many safety incidents have occurred there in the last three years. You're going to have all the data about all those people's body sensors. Not to get too creepy, but in some organizations you may have full video and audio of everything said and done. That's just in *one room* of your headquarters building.

This is amazing and slightly overwhelming, but it has big implications for your advisors—even your lawyers, medical consultants, and accountants—when it comes to how you use it. They're going to have access to a massive volume of usable data, both inside and outside your organization, either through open data sets or publicly available data that scrubs the specifics about individuals and personal details (we hope).

Bottom line: your ability to store, access, and share legally collected and historical data with your advisors is going to grow rapidly.

The *cost* to actually get your hands on that data inside and outside of your company is going to collapse. The need for direct observation, time studies, interviews, and similar primary consulting research will become much easier once infrastructure is in place. That means direct measure costs drop with the proliferation of sensors and the Internet of Things and your ability to simply buy data that you don't already have.

UBIQUITOUS AND UNLIMITED DATA

It's hard to fully explain how big data has changed the way consulting works—and it's really all behind the scenes for most clients. Organizations expect that data collection—which was at one time one of our main jobs—isn't even a topic of discussion, much less something we get paid for. It's not even always clear where data comes from, as Microsliced services functions share data so seamlessly, from different sources for customized solutions. For quite some time, this presented some serious data quality problems, because organizations started to assume that data, if shared through trusted applications, could automatically be trusted. After some high-profile embarrassments—especially in the early 2020s—specialized applications that assessed and "scored" the quality of blended data sets dramatically improved the usefulness of data that was very hard to trace.

///

I know that this all sounds fantastic—but here's the thing about big data. Big data by itself is not enough to enable Microslices as defined in this book. In fact, big sets of data are pretty *stupid* by themselves (which is one of the reasons I abhor the term). Data needs *insight* so that it can be transformed into knowledge that can be used.

With this kind of data volume, data scientists need some big time firepower to make it useful. In the words of *Jaws* police chief Martin Brody, "You're gonna need a bigger boat."

Processing Power per Dollar, AI, and Machine Learning

Fundamental to the organization and realization of the Microslices model is the ability for advisors to deal with the explosion of data. Sure, we can collect and store it. But without the second of the three technologies necessary for Microslices—the processing power to automate the interpretation of all that data—it's meaningless.

You can hire an army of data scientists, but they simply could not have gotten through today's data with the technologies that we had five or ten years ago. The tools and applications we have today are certainly far better—the laptop I'm typing on right now is probably about ten times more powerful than the one I was using five years ago—but they must keep pace with the vast array of articles, emails, spreadsheets, video, audio, and other data generated every second of every day in my clients' organizations to be helpful. As I mentioned in the last chapter, that's why data scientists are far more than dressed-up statisticians—they require skills in computer science, programming, and even digital design to attack the monstrous and growing body of data in every field imaginable.

In the 1990s and 2000s, the focus of automation was primarily on brute force filtering. This boiled down to sifting through mountains of data so that humans could then look at some subset of things that might be meaningful. This was a topic of regular conversation even when I started at the CIA as a young analyst in 1995. As human analysts, how could we possibly sift through the volume of information we had available to us? How could we possibly look at all of those satellite photos—especially when there was a new private company taking satellite photos, too? On top of all that, how in the world could we cross-reference all of it with everything else? At the time, we hoped that computing would help us simply "down-select" some of it.

Here's a practical example from my former employers at Langley. It comes from the wildly successful CORONA satellite program that ran from 1960 to 1972.[27] The United States launched 121 "units" or cameras over that period. The most advanced of those cameras, the J-3, accounted for 17 of those 121; from orbit, the J-3 could spot objects just five feet wide (which was pretty spectacular accuracy at the time). The program produced "2 million linear shelf-feet" of satellite images—which was then a massive volume. Today, Digital Globe, a commercial imagery company, photographs 3 million square kilometers of the earth—per day. There aren't enough light tables for that. Or eyeballs. Machines are a necessity.

During the 1990s and 2000s, when companies and governments needed to evaluate these photos—to look for oil fields, roads, or bad guys—the goal would be to use brute force to select the 1,000 or 2,000 photos that the human analyst could look at and interpret. But that proved impractical. There's just too much data, too many images—even after all the sifting that we can do—for us meager humans to deal with.

The key part of our inability to process that amount of data is that we can't connect the dots between sifted facts of disparate data sets ourselves. The key to both unlocking the insights from data—and connecting them to insights in other data sets—is to accelerate increases in processing power. Some might call this "exponential" growth in processing power, but let's just say the performance curve is steep and getting steeper. While processing power itself—CPU speed, for example—isn't AI or machine learning or natural language processing, processing power is the

27 | CIA History Staff, Center for the Study of Intelligence, Kevin C. Ruffner, editor, *CORONA: America's First Spy Satellite Program* (1995).

fundamental precursor technology that expands the aggregate capacity of a system to process information and interpret it.

Coming back to professional services and consulting in particular, human advisors have been in the same pickle as those CIA imagery analysts so many years ago. As you know, your advisors need complete information to provide the right advice. But how in the world are they going to handle that when the volume of information is so great—when the volume of information available on any particular topic doubles every couple of years?

Accelerating growth in computing power will allow machines to draw richer conclusions from small and large data sets, both structured and unstructured, and replace many analytical and interpretive functions currently performed by consultants.

Enter the fascinating disciplines of artificial intelligence (AI) and machine learning. I'm not saying that robots are going to replace your consultants in every case. I am saying that AI is getting stronger and is going to have a profound impact on the business of advice giving. The September 2014 issue of *McKinsey Quarterly* goes as far as to say that we've hit the vertical part of the machine learning curve[28]—which means change will now happen far *faster* than it has over the last ten years.

Increased processing power, using on-demand computational processing, cloud resources, or sometimes local resources, will be more than capable of reading those unstructured data sets—and drawing accurate and very rapid conclusions about the health of a division in your company, the bottlenecks in a process, or the

---

28 | Computers are replacing skilled practitioners in fields such as architecture, aviation, the law, medicine, and petroleum geology—and changing the nature of work in a broad range of other jobs and professions.

morale of a team, all using computers and distributed data collection from humans in your organization.

What's more, that same processing power can cross-reference those conclusions against data sets you already have, about things like employee health and the locations of trucks and inventory, and further corroborate the machine's conclusions. In our case studies section, I show two examples of this kind of innovation in use today—representing the future of the advice-giving business.

If AI can do all that, it starts to sound a whole lot like what your consultant is doing for you now. This is not the plot of some movie or wild speculation by starry-eyed science fiction enthusiasts. It is real. AI is getting much better at tasks that some might consider too creative or unstructured for a machine. Clay Christensen's critique of consulting explicitly points to computing power changing the consulting game—he goes as far as predicting the complete obsolescence of the junior analyst.

Still, we are in a period where we are witnessing machines just beginning to tackle "human-like" challenges. That's a far cry from strong AI or machine intelligence, but it is a step in that direction. If the trend holds up, those of us in the advice business are in for a wild ride, because the distinction between what a "trusted advisor" does and what a machine does will blur significantly.

Notable Predictions by Ray Kurzweil

- By the late 2010s, ten terabytes of computing power (roughly the same as the human brain) will cost about $1,000.

- By the 2020s, most diseases will go away as nanobots become smarter than current medical technology.

- By 2045, we will multiply our intelligence a billionfold by linking wirelessly from our neocortex to a synthetic neocortex in the cloud.

Source: Peter Diamandis interview with Ray Kurzweil: http://singularityhub.com/2015/01/26/ray-kurzweils-mind-boggling-predictions-for-the-next-25-years/

Notable Predictions by Erik Brynjolffson

- In the next 24 months, the planet will add more computer power than it did in all previous history.

- Over the next 24 years, the increase will likely be over a thousand-fold.

- Within our lifetimes, we will likely create true machine intelligence and the connection of all humans via a common digital network

Citation: *The Second Machine Age*

In the chart above, you can see a lot of notable, intelligent, thoughtful people making some fairly bold, even radical predictions—terrifying for some, exciting for others—about the implications of rapidly improving computing power.

But why should we believe this is really going to happen? After all, we're still waiting on those flying cars. It's our natural human inclination to view progress *linearly*, when in fact (in aggregate) technological progress has always followed a *logarithmic* pattern. The most famous description of this pattern is Moore's Law, discussed earlier in this chapter. Originally meaning that the number of transistors you could get on a chip would double every two years, Moore's Law is now broadly used to refer to this general pattern of technology advancement, in which relative performance per dollar doubles every 18 months to two years.

However, for the pace of technology change to continue, computer scientists will have to overcome some serious physics problems. Advanced technologies like quantum computing and graphene processors hold promise in keeping the pace of change going. Despite these daunting challenges, remember that a lot of people have predicted the demise of Moore's Law in the past 40 years. They base their objections on size. Or heat. Or power. It could be limits of physics that we didn't understand. So far, every one of these naysayers has been wrong. Every single one.

I won't be one of the people who predicts the end of exponential technology growth. Even if processing speed per dollar takes twice as long to double as it does today, consulting is still going to be fundamentally changed in the next 10 to 15 years. The pace of change is so rapid it's a little hard to even know what the future is going to look like. It's going to be very different in 2025 and 2030—and so different that I don't think even the most gifted futurist can predict what will come afterward.

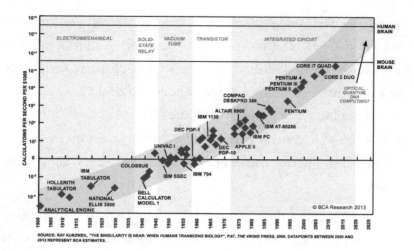

Computing power and big data sets are a big deal. But just applying them to isolated problems would make their use impractical for Microslices—this means that all types of advice giving will be compressed, specialized, and automated. If that's going to happen, computing power and data sets need to be able to hook together quickly and adaptively to solve problems. If every problem is a unique quilt of circumstances, we need something to stitch together that quilt.

Application Innovation or How Open APIs Made Me Handsome and Popular

The third of the three technologies that are so crucial to the advance of Microslices is application innovation, which builds on, enhances, and connects other technologies. The terms that define this phenomenon are many and varied; IBM calls it the "innovation economy." Some have called it the "API economy." Some have called it the "sharing economy." What's important is that the facilitation of interfaces between both complex and simple applications is expanding *just as rapidly as the technologies themselves*. These interfaces and how they are used enables—in ways that we don't yet fully understand—the networked delivery model of Microslices.

Certainly big data and AI have been well-documented drivers of change in professional services. However, those technologies can't realize their potential unless they can be "hung together" with meaningful connectivity. "Connectivity" for a long time has meant network interfaces, but that's only a small part of the story.

Specifically, open application programming interfaces (open APIs) and the proliferation of light, connected, and niche applications that replace parts of the consulting process are the third critical enabling technology development behind Microslices. Why? Because they are like language to humans. Each of us is uniquely capable, creative, and talented in our own way—but without language, humans would be isolated and unable to learn. Open APIs to computing are like speech to humans—they allow smart, well-designed and creative machines to communicate with each other, which allows them to learn from and enhance one another.

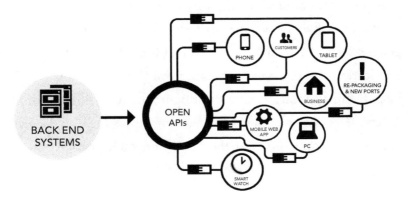

IBM's Jerry Cuomo estimates that by 2016 the number of open APIs will hit 30,000. Paralleling the views in this book, Cuomo thinks that explosive growth can make smaller, niche players more competitive in ways that we don't even know about yet. For those of you new to APIs, let's just stipulate that 30,000[29] is a lot of open APIs. If the number doubles every 18 to 24 months—and I believe it will—then by 2025 the number of open APIs will be in the neighborhood of 1 million.

A practical example of the growth and importance of open APIs can be found as close as your nearest browser. If you use any of Basecamp's[30] products (Basecamp or Highrise, for example) or you're a Salesforce or Quickbooks user, open APIs allow all those little applications to plug into each other. Enterprise applications with which you're already very familiar make significant use of APIs, although they aren't all open APIs and are used not only to allow applications to work together but to draw together "walled gardens" of applications purpose-built for a particular enterprise product.

Crack open your laptop and go to your enterprise application of choice. If it's a pretty good one, you'll find somewhere a list of "integrations." In the list on that page, there used to be only four or five. Now, you just keep scrolling, with too many to get through. There are 20, 150, or 200 of those things per one application. It's pretty neat, because you can plug in any number of different applications and reconfigure them to different things. A few years ago, everyone talked about "app stores." Now, every app has an app store, and they build on each other to provide

29 | Jerry Cuomo, "Why the Growing API Economy Gives Developers Limitless Opportunities." VentureBeat, July 2, 2014.
http://venturebeat.com/2014/07/02/api-economy-developers/

30 | Basecamp is the company formerly known as 37Signals.

a rich, interconnected set of capabilities within whichever app you're working with.

This is not new. Application mash-ups have been around for a while. What is new is the notion that applications and data sets, enabled by enhanced computational power, can assemble themselves rapidly around a unique problem and solution. In other words, instead of one application providing an answer, it automatically (via open APIs) leverages the unique "skills" of a host of specialist applications.

For example, if you're a user of both Uber and OpenTable, you can book a car right from the OpenTable app on your phone. What you don't see in the background is how the handoffs occur between these applications in real time to solve your specific, niche problem (in this case, booking a car directly from a restaurant). This networked model of delivering applications is a lot like what we're describing in Microslices—a networked model of delivering consulting services.

In some circumstances, this approach is similar to contextual computing. Contextual computing today does this with apps that already exist so that when you walk into a certain building, your smartphone knows that you're there and makes you a recommendation based on physical proximity.

In an example with which you're already familiar, Google Now (which most Android users are familiar with) can notify you when a nearby retail store is offering a sale on something you searched for online. Google Now advises the user of information that's relevant to their location.[31]

Proliferating and smarter open APIs make this much cooler. Applications may be able to leverage AI, machine learning, and open APIs to solve problems not previously encountered. If you have a robust, diverse set of networked applications that provide niche advice, the APIs to connect them, and very high computational speed, applications could "self-assemble."

In a simple example of retail, an application like Google Now might know that:

(a) the user is a man,

(b) he's walking into a ladies' store,

(c) he's not shopping for himself (so he's likely shopping for his girlfriend), and

(d) his girlfriend has only been in his contacts database for two weeks.

Based on all that, the application might recommend a dress that's on sale and not the lingerie.

To take that scenario further, if data had already been collected—or if his smartphone was linked to his girlfriend's previous purchase and search data—it could know her size, her color preferences, and what style of dress is best for her body type and be able to guide the man to a dress that would be abso-

31 | Chris Welch, "Google Now will tell you if nearby stores have a product you've searched for," May 5, 2014, http://www.theverge.com/2014/5/5/5684634/google-now-tracks-if-nearby-store-has-product-you-searched-for

lutely perfect for her. Furthermore, it might review his calendar and learn that he hasn't seen her in several months, so the gift had better be *good*. Finally, it knows that the store has the dress on sale 75 yards from your location in stock, in her size, in her favorite color, and is on a specific shelf and can direct you to that dress using augmented reality on your phone's screen or personal heads-up display device. In short, there's a lot going on to make a simple recommendation.

Why couldn't Google Now (or something like it) advise a regional executive when a plant he's about to visit has been under- or overperforming, and why? In this case, rather than knowing that a customer is at a store to shop for his girlfriend, it would know that the executive is going to Wichita because the plant there has been performing poorly. Rather than recommending a dress, it might direct the executive to focus on the cross-docking facility at the plant, because the vast amount of product data— which is automatically collected continuously—suggests a spike in front-end inventory.

Or why couldn't the user be a general in the Air Force, visiting an installation? Typically, a staffer or a consultant would prepare PowerPoint slides regarding which locations to visit and what questions to ask. But using APIs, the general could be provided contextual information that pulled together current information from a variety of enterprise systems, other advisors, geography, weather, and other data—from both public and private sources and both public and commercial tools.

The above examples illustrate a customized scenario created for a particular person that didn't exist before. You need a lot of computing power to do that. You need a lot of applications, and you need a lot of open APIs. The good news is that development of APIs is fairly easy to do and getting easier. Phil Simon, author of *The Age of the Platform*, perhaps says it best:

> *Custom APIs are no longer the sole purview of very large corporations. It's never been more affordable for small businesses and mid-market organizations to do these types of things, a trend that shows no signs of abating. I'd also argue that these types of considerations have become more essential than ever. Every company is becoming a tech company; some just haven't realized it yet.*[32]

The pace of applications developed and deployed that can leverage this data and computing power is accelerating rapidly. But applications are becoming more and more "lightweight," which reduces complexity and makes deployment of new tools a hell of a lot less painful.

Traditional tools like enterprise software are mind-numbingly complex to both deploy and use; they try to do too many things and provide too much functionality. A lightweight application is one that is both simply designed and very narrow in scope. In my own company, we have moved away from enterprise systems that "do everything" to a collection of connected, niche products like Slack (for communications), Google Drive (for storage), Hubspot (for marketing), Asana (for project management), and Harvest (for expenses). We also resist the urge to try to make simple tools "better" by adding features.

---

32 | Phil Simon, "Proprietary APIs: A New Tool in the Age of Platform," October 28, 2014, http://www.huffingtonpost.com/phil-simon/proprietary-apis-a-new-to_b_6061722.html

Don't forget about networking—and security. For all of those sensors, audio/video feeds, and routine corporate network applications to function, they must be connected. I'm not talking about the wires and switches of today but the underlying protocols therein. Things like IPv6. Every one of the technologies mentioned here requires connectivity. With each other, with other systems, within themselves. The Internet of Things/Internet of Everything will not be possible without connectivity. Big data means big data transport. Connectivity from the data center to the home and to the mobile individual and to every device everywhere will be even more critical in the future. In addition, disruptions to that connectivity would be devastating, increasing the need for significant and widely accessible cybersecurity and information security technology.

We consume some of these applications now at the user interface layer—the part we see and touch—but there are a plethora of discrete applications and algorithms working behind the scenes. Applications are just collections of code to solve a problem, and these are shrinking in scope, even as their bundling and layering allows the user interface to appear broader in scope. Siri and Google Now seem like magic, but they are just the interface layer on a collusion of specialized tools—related to maps, retail data, inventory projections, search history, browsers, and demographic analysis—that are becoming ever more specialized.

Professional services is evolving in a similar pattern. Instead of hiring a behemoth firm to do everything, you'll have a "user interface layer" that may be a firm or a tool. And the specialized work—from organizational structure analysis, to strategy, to pricing, to demand forecasting, to process optimization—will be completed by a network of niche specialists delivering together.

The exponential growth that Moore's Law elegantly demonstrates is not just about chips and processing speed and data. It's also about applications, packages, APIs, and combinations thereof.

In another example of how small, niche tools assemble to solve problems, Netflix published an article in June 2014 demonstrating that increasingly small blocks from niche problems are solved by niche processors, which organize themselves to form a complex system without any intervention from engineers.

> *The hypothesis is that complex systems can be built efficiently if they are reduced to small, local problems that are solved in relative isolation with processors. These small blocks are then automatically assembled to reveal a fully formed system. Such a system would no longer require engineers to understand their entire scope before making significant contributions. These systems would be free to scale without taxing their engineering teams proportionally. Likewise, their teams could grow without investing in lots of onboarding time for each new member.[33]*

This example of problem/solution pairs is a whole lot like a Microslice in the consulting model of the future. If applications that solve very narrow problems explode and enable open APIs, those in turn will self-assemble to solve complex problems. Seemingly disparate consulting Microslices will be bundled to solve a very, very complex problem. Talk about cool.

33 | Nicholas Eddy, "Building Netflix Payback with Self-Assembling Components," June 2, 2014, http://techblog.netflix.com/2014/06/building-netflix-playback-with-self.html

OPEN APIS LET MACHINES "HUG"

The easiest way I can explain application development and open APIs in 2030 is to remind you of the way we all migrated from DOS to Windows to Gesture and natural language interfaces. It started out as code and became visual and in turn became intuitive. If something is intuitive, it's accessible to everyone. "Application development" in 2030 is something just about everyone does—it's just not happening in a programming interface anymore. In addition, the vast leaps in processing and AI mean that machines help us dynamically assemble these applications to solve problems. Applications are also building applications (assembled from increasingly specialized applications) automatically.

//

What These Technology Trends Mean for Professional Services

So what does all of this mean for consulting?

As explained at the outset of this book, Microslices is a business model for professional services that, in part, requires the automation of increasingly specialized consulting activities. The impact of that automation is significant. Imagine a very realistic future when computing power is used for seamless language processing and complex self-direction of problem solving, pointed at a consulting problem. That routine interaction we take for granted—*asking a question*—would conceivably be partially or even largely replaced by a "black box" that understands you, then uses hundreds of APIs and hundreds of thousands of data points to provide an answer.

A study released by the McKinsey Global Institute[34] predicts that between now and 2025, the impact of automation on knowledge work *alone* will be between $5.2 and $6.7 trillion dollars worldwide. That is a "T"—*trillion*.

It's exciting, and perhaps unsettling, to envision the possible applications for such automation.

Imagine having a potential lawsuit on your hands and being able to consult a computer to determine the probability of being able to win the lawsuit—just by explaining or inputting the data pertaining to your case. The application might also let you know if it's worth going to court or pursuing a settlement. For a senior defense policymaker, just think of a future where you could describe your desired outcomes for a procurement, and a system outlines the top potential offerors, estimates the price and delivery timeframe, and prebuilds an RFP for release. It might even predict the outcome of the procurement and recommend the best option.

Big data, significant advancement and computing power, and networks of API-connected tools can make these scenarios a reality.

The three technologies outlined above, while not the *only* technologies that enable Microslices, reinforce and accelerate each other in a way that is the key to the current and coming shift in professional services. As computing power and AI improve, those tools can be applied to large data sets, which in turn can be applied to solve API architecture problems. Computer scientists will work on machine learning challenges using more applications

34 | James Manyika, Michael Chui, Jacques Bughin, Richard Dobbs, Peter Bisson, and Alex Marrs, "Disruptive technologies: Advances that will transform life, business, and the global economy." McKinsey Global Institute, May 2013. http://www.mckinsey.com/insights/business_technology/disruptive_technologies

connected by better open APIs, which will give them better computational speed to solve different kinds of open API problems. It is, in short, a virtuous cycle of innovation.

There will be a constant cycle of technologies reinforcing each other and applying themselves to a variety of other Microslice-enabling technologies, like speech recognition, sensor development, logistics, and information analysis.

Microslicing begets more Microslicing

The growth of technology is a fundamental enabler for this new business model of advice giving. Technology also enables growth and productivity in our economy, despite some prognostication that technology can be a permanent job killer. The exponential curve we're surfing right now in technology will manifest itself in new business models like Microslices—but in other industries as well. Just as we're seeing tech curves bend up and get faster and faster and faster, we'll see business model innovation get faster and faster and faster.

The idea of all this data and all these solutions coming faster and faster, delivered by smarter and smarter technology, may have you asking, "Is the reward for all this a shorter workweek? Will we only have to go to work for four hours to accomplish what we need to accomplish in a week? What will happen to all those white-collar knowledge workers?" You might even fear for the jobs of your consultants (and you know it will be bad if it comes to that).

There are two camps on the issue of technology-driven job displacement. One is alarmist, led by those who are convinced that we're going to end up angry and unemployed and that we'll turn violent and tear down our own technology. (I'm not making that up—there are some very serious, very smart people in that camp.) Solutions offered vary from carefully controlled intervention and regulation to alternative economic schemes that centrally plan or allocate resources in new ways.[35]

The other camp, which I believe is on the right side of history, is more optimistic about the future of jobs and productivity and skeptical of one-size-fits-all plans to prevent displacement of jobs. The optimist camp contends that experts are pretty bad at allocating resources or understanding what new kinds of jobs and what new kinds of opportunities new technologies uncover. In fact, as our technology, economy, and culture becomes more and more diverse, fast moving, and complex, it may be fundamentally flawed to assume that any expert or group of experts can possibly comprehend the problem, much less the solution, to disruption in the economy caused by these shifts.

As we know today, but could not fathom at the time, entire economic subsystems developed from the disruption of the news and publishing industries. The automobile killed the horse and buggy but in turn created an entirely new way of working, living, and communicating. Is the pace of change faster? Yes. However, I believe that our culture—and even our governments—will adapt to the pace of change. The self-organization of the economy, without heavy-handed experimentation, will continue to prove the most efficient way of creating jobs and opportunities, not just for knowledge workers but for all workers.

Just because we can't conceive of what the future will hold doesn't mean the world is ending. While many have uncovered pieces of the puzzle, nobody knows for sure. I don't know. Ray Kurzweil, Peter Diamandis, and their racquetball team at Singularity University don't know. Clayton Christensen and his friends at Harvard don't know.

35 | Jaron Lanier. *Who Owns the Future?* New York: Simon & Schuster, 2013.

Even with the proliferation of data science at our fingertips and the technology to deliver it, we are still faced with the same human dilemma when it comes to guessing what the future holds. Honestly, we won't know until we get there, but you can count on there being new and different opportunities to work on when we do.

THE MANY DIMENSIONS OF MOORE'S LAW

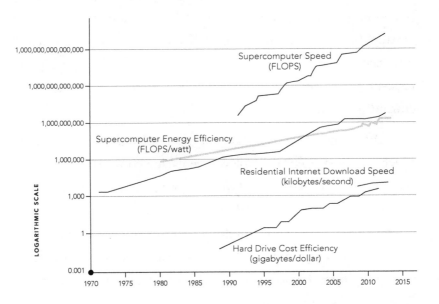

GRAPH ADAPTED FROM ERIK BRYNJOLFSSON AND ANDREW MCAFEE, *THE SECOND MACHINE AGE: WORK, PROGRESS, AND PROSPERITY IN A TIME OF BRILLIANT TECHNOLOGIES*. W. W. NORTON & COMPANY, 2014.

This Isn't about Tech; It's about How Tech Changes How Services Are Bought

What happens when the shiny new technology that we're talking about here actually replaces the advisor who recommended it? That's a critical issue and an implication of this technology on Microslices and what it means for you.

The technology described won't just transform your business; it will also transform your consultants and advisors. The advisors cannot limit themselves to understanding the importance of technology for *you*. They need to understand the importance of technology for *themselves* and how to use it to deliver their results to you. How is this going to play out? The really significant effects of these technologies in consulting, law, and professional services are only going to be apparent in very niche functions at first. That's already the case in law and finance. We see it now with automated financial advice being given by tools like WealthFront and paralegal-like activities being performed by systems. And we see it in consulting as well.

Over time, executives like you will not be able to ignore how much is gained from niche players replacing consulting tasks with specialized automation, and you're going to want more. You're going to want more Microslices. You're going to look for more opportunities to apply technology to automate consulting tasks, because you can get more scale. While machines are far away from replacing human knowledge work completely, they are much faster, and the advice is increasingly reliable.

Luckily for us, that doesn't mean there won't be humans involved. There will be more jobs that can be done by machines instead of people, but if you're equipped with the knowledge about what these technologies are, and what they mean, then you are in as good a position as you can be. In fact, just being aware of the situation has already placed you in a stronger position to apply the coming changes to the survival of your own organization.

If you're feeling worried about robots taking over our lives and thousands of cameras and sensors recording our every move, think back on the terror people felt—people just like you and me—at switching from lamps lit with whale oil to lamps lit with electric bulbs. Or the end-time predictions that shook households across the nation when telephones were first installed. It is in our nature to resist the unknown. New waves of technology have always been met with trepidation. And still time marches on. Keep your fears at bay and so will you.

That's why the final chapter in part I of this book focuses on culture, not your organizational culture or company culture, but the fundamental shift underway in our national (and international) culture. This cultural shift is the third critically important enabler of Microslices covered in this book.

- ○ Tech is a crucial enabler of Microslices and the future of professional services.

- ○ This isn't new—technology and consulting have always walked hand in hand.

- ○ However, three current technology developments are set to change professional services forever.

- ○ Big data, computing power and AI, and APIs are the three most important among many crucial technologies for Microslices.

- ○ Big data promises you and your consulting providers a mind-boggling amount of information that doubles every two years.

- ○ Computing power is fueling AI and machine learning, which can unlock big data's potential.

- ○ Open APIs are the connective tissue that will allow small, specialized applications—and small, specialized consultants—to rapidly assemble customized services and solutions.

- ○ These technologies together create a cycle of innovation that will accelerate their development and in turn accelerate the pace of change in consulting business models.

//

THE DRIVING FORCES— MILLENNIAL CULTURE

True terror is to wake up one morning and discover that your high school class is running the country.

–Kurt Vonnegut

efore moving on, let's recap: The first driving force we talked about is data science. Data science—and our ability to creatively collect, analyze, and communicate data—is critical to enabling the Microslices consulting model.

The second driving force is technology—specifically, the three technologies that most facilitate the compression, automation, and specialization of professional services.

One might be tempted to stop there and say, "Well, that's enough. It's really about technology and data science." But that would miss the significant—and difficult—mind shift required for organizations and executives to adopt the Microslices model. As you know from managing your own organization, a big part of being a quantitative organization, or adopting advanced technology, is change management. If you were reading the last chapter and were feeling a little overwhelmed and tired by the end of it, then you have an inkling of how it's going to feel to try and adapt an organization.

To adapt—and to coach the other people in your company through that change—you must understand the cultural shift that accompanies it. Do not underestimate the importance of cultural change management. While many organizations will adopt the data science and technology described in previous chapters, they will lose to their competitors if they don't understand and embrace the attitudes outlined in this chapter.

The third driving force of Microslices is the "millennial attitude": an innate trust of technology, valuing results over activity, and a bias for experimentation.

By now you've been subjected to a steady drumbeat of trendy articles and infographics about millennials as a generation. The millennial *attitude* isn't just a cultural trend, or yet another generalization about how your youngest workers think. The millennial attitude, in the context of Microslices, will change the way executives buy consulting and professional services. Why? Because those with a millennial attitude are uniquely prepared to adapt to

Microslices and its completely different approach to consuming advice from outside the organization.

By using the term "millennial attitude" I am not referring to a specific age range but about cultural norms typified by an age range. There's nothing special about people born after 1980. But there is a cultural and attitudinal effect of growing up with an iPhone in your hand and the Internet always within reach. Millennials don't know a world without text messaging. They have always had most of the world's knowledge at their fingertips. They have never used a phone book or gone to the store to buy a new album on its release date. That changes their cultural attitudes toward timeliness, technology, information, science, math, and results.

The bottom line is that Microslices can't happen without the right preferences, perceptions, and attitudes in place. Fortunately, they're on the rise.

If you as a CEO—and the managers who work in the organization—reject or resist the idea of changing the way advice is purchased and consumed by the organization, Microslices won't take hold in your organization. But the *next* generation of organization leaders may not perceive the world as you do. At 45, they'll still be 45, but they'll still be millennials. They will have grown up with strings in their hands and the world's knowledge at their fingertips. This chapter isn't about the culture of a certain age group, because anyone of any age can have a millennial attitude. In light of that, you as an executive have two imperatives with regard to cultural change:

1. You must understand what a millennial attitude is, because it's the "default setting" of everyone in your organization born after 1980.

2. You must learn how everyone of all ages in your organization can adopt the best aspects of the millennial attitude.

The Ingredients of a Millennial Attitude

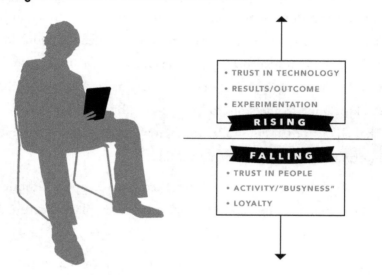

- TRUST IN TECHNOLOGY
- RESULTS/OUTCOME
- EXPERIMENTATION

RISING

FALLING

- TRUST IN PEOPLE
- ACTIVITY/"BUSYNESS"
- LOYALTY

For the purposes of this book and with regard to how this cultural trend defines Microslices, a millennial attitude has three key ingredients:

1. Shifting trust from *people* to *technology*

2. An insistence on *results* rather than *activity*

3. A bias for frequent *experimentation* rather than *long-term loyalty*

Let's break these down one at a time.

First, those with a millennial attitude have relatively low trust in other human beings, while having relatively high trust in technology. This is important for professional services, because trust has always been the critical ingredient in successful advice giving. Millennials are half as likely as baby boomers to agree with the statement that "most people can be trusted."[36] Conversely, they are far more likely to rapidly adopt new technology like smartphones, wearables, and gaming platforms and far less likely to use PCs and traditional phones than other demographic groups.[37]

The move away from being face-to-face has become mainstream because of the way millennials interact with technology. They trust results appearing on their phone. They don't mind that the customer service rep they're chatting with may be an AI.

Second, those with a millennial attitude expect results, not activity or "busyness." In simple terms, that often translates into convenience; they want the desired result as quickly and efficiently as possible and have limited tolerance for dues paying, bureaucracy, or complex rules. They shop for groceries at convenience stores twice as often as non-millennials and even make donations to charities using their mobile device at three times the rate of non-millennials.[38] Some would mistakenly label this behavior as laziness; in fact, it is an expectation of efficiency and speed and a preference for simplification.

This group expects results quickly and often for free (especially for information). They're not used to having to pay for online content. In fact, the idea of paying for opinions seems almost absurd to many millennials, which complicates the concept of selling them knowledge.

36 | Pew Research Center, "Millennials in Adulthood: Detached from Institutions, Networked with Friends," March, 2014

37 | Christine Barton, Jeff Fromm, and Chris Egan, "The Millennial Consumer: Debunking Stereotypes," Boston Consulting Group, April 2012

38 | Ibid.

In turn, the combination of technology adoption and a results orientation drives millennial thinkers to readily adopt connections with others driven by technology: social media. Not only does that mean that they rely on technology to facilitate "personal" interaction but that they feel that technology *enriches* personal connections. They in turn are more likely to contribute to technology-enabled communities to both give and receive advice, more likely to contribute user-generated content, and more likely to be members of social networking sites and mobile communities.[39] Physical proximity to the people and technologies that provide that advice isn't important.

This focus on results has enormous implications for how they will buy advice and professional services. Millennial thinkers' insistence on speed and results, rather than long, hourly billed projects, will force advisors to change both their sales and delivery methods.

Third, millennial thinkers are far more likely to conduct frequent experiments than others, affecting their loyalty to brands, advisors, technologies, and other products and services. The most striking example is their lack of attachment to traditional religious and political institutions; this reluctance to attach to institutions reflects a general preference toward experimentation. Those with a millennial attitude believe that the technology employed by a product or service is the most important factor in remaining loyal.[40] In other words, if your tech isn't up to date, a millennial

39 | "Beyond digital: connecting media and entertainment to the future," IBM, 2012.

40 | Natalie Tadena, "For Millennials, Use of Technology Just as Important as Brand Name, Study Finds," Janary 27, 2015,

http://blogs.wsj.com/cmo/2015/01/27/

for-millennials-use-of-technology-just-as-important-as-brand-name-study-finds/

thinker will show you the door. As millennials enter the C-suite and their attitudes permeate your organization, this willingness to switch technologies and experiment with new ones will change their thinking on buying professional services.

My company, Big Sky, has placed at the core of its strategy and hiring the idea that we must all become millennial thinkers. Big Sky has a physically dispersed workforce with no central office. We don't track hours and have unlimited vacation. We connect with each other with technology far more than we connect with each other in person—and our culture is incredibly strong. Big Skyers don't see each other physically very much, but we have an incredibly close-knit, family feel. Being able to work when they want, wherever they want is very attractive to millennial-minded people who expect a lot of convenience and power over their lives.

Big Sky has a millennial mindset, but we aren't all millennials. We trust technology and switch tools and platforms frequently if it helps us or our clients. We juggle multiple applications simulta-neously. Instant messaging, chat rooms, video chat, social task and project management tools, and a variety of other techniques keep us in sync and connected. We treat our employees like adults and extend them every trust and convenience as long as results are met. Most importantly, Big Skyers *deliver* for their clients. Most of the firms that I grew up in would not have been able to achieve a tight culture without being physically present, and yet Big Sky is doing it.

The Millennial Attitude as an Enabler of Microslices

Without that cultural shift, Microslices would be impossible. Organizations will not reap the benefits of Microslices without a culture that demands results, trusts science and technology, and is willing to experiment.

An investment banker friend of mine in Charlotte, North Carolina, has a son who is about ten years old. The kid recently asked his dad, "How old is Drew Brees?" The dad replied, "33, I think." His kid looked at him skeptically and then pulled out a smartphone and asked it, "Okay Google. How old is Drew Brees?" The phone answered, "36." Who do you think the kid believed? The father who welcomed him at birth, changed his diapers, fed him, and provided him shelter? Or the $250 phone? News flash: He believed the phone.

Our culture is changing. Very accurate information can be had very cheaply and very quickly. This is an important development for Microslices because it changes consultants and the way they must behave. More importantly, it will change *you*. By "you," I mean the person sitting in the executive's seat, who buys advice. Because if you're not a millennial or you don't have a millennial attitude, the person who comes behind you is likely already thinking this way.

In 2030 the oldest millennials, born in 1980, will be 50. Their attitude toward technology is going to be dominant over the next 15 to 20 years. In 2015, the oldest millennials are about 35. Given the way millennial thinkers interact with information, what does that mean for your company or government?

It means your organization is going to change, fundamentally. All those traits outlined above—wanting information for free, not trusting institutions but trusting technology, demanding results— they're going to change the way your company buys professional services, which is crucial for both you and the consulting industry.

MILLENNIAL ATTITUDES
OF BUYERS AND SELLERS

ACTIVITY	BUYER	SELLER
RESULTS ORIENTATION	Wants a result now and wants to pay a price for that result. Doesn't care how you're doing it.	Doesn't care when or where they work or how long it takes. They're willing to be paid for the result.
TIMELESSNESS	Doesn't want to be constrained by meeting schedules, delivery team member timelines, or take on new employee hours.	Doesn't like a 9-5 work environment.
TECHNOLOGY ADOPTION	Adopts technology very quickly.	EXPECTS all tech to be continuously updated to latest and greatest.
TRUST	Trust technology more than outside advisors.	Reluctant to sell services based on relationships.
PERCEPTION OF MACHINE INTELLIGENCE	Content to accept the judgment of an algorithm.	Can quickly shift personal knowledge into tools.

There are two sides in a negotiation between millennial thinkers—one that wants to pay for results and another that wants to get paid for results. As a millennial executive, you want a result right now. You logically conclude that to get that result the organization should pay a specific price, and you don't care how it gets done. Meanwhile, the millennial seller—consultant, lawyer, doctor, or accountant—doesn't want to be bothered with when, or where they physically work to deliver that result or how long it's taking them. They just want to be fulfilled by doing a great job and to get paid for it.

This also means that consulting firms will have to scale their businesses and the products they offer. They may need 100 clients to make the same money they make from one client today. They may need to build apps that present their advice and knowledge in a highly consumable format. We'll look at that in more depth in chapters to come.

As you can see in the table above, the attitudes of millennials, applied to buying and selling consulting or other professional services, challenge basic assumptions about the traditional delivery model. The old system is not going to work with millennial thinkers, especially with the technology and data science they have available as described in chapters 2 and 3.

The trends I've described don't just apply to consulting clients and executives like you; they apply to everyone—McKinsey, Deloitte, and BCG all the way down to niche specialists like Big Sky. What should give the established professional services firms pause is being the last to adopt a millennial attitude. It's not enough to hire a clown car full of 25-year-old MBAs and declare victory; it is critical that even the most experienced leaders of every firm change their mindsets.

As with technological disruptive innovation, it is likely that the cultural disruption associated with Microslices will be pioneered by niche players. Large, successful firms have a proven inherent disadvantage in adapting within their current customer service models—and within themselves. It's up to the executive buyer of professional services to discern which firms "get it" and which don't.

This will play out in obvious ways, such as resistance to advanced automation of advice, which is already in its early stages with systems like IBM's Boardroom Watson. No matter how good the advice is or how much time it saves, devotees of the traditional model of buying professional services will resist. They will do so in the face of measurable proof, logic, and good sense. Your job is to not be that customer.

But the reality is, once the cultural shift starts to overcome the naysayers, Microslices is going to stick. The technology needs to be there. The data science needs to be there. But as executives focus less on traditional service delivery—and more on technology-enabled advice—Microslices will become dominant.

FROM FAD TO FOUNDATION

Firms that adopted Microslices or other alternative delivery models were a bit slow to start in 2014-2016 and were focused on narrow applications. The culture of both clients and consultants shifted dramatically, mirroring the rest of the economy. Professional services like law, consulting, and even medicine became dominated in the mid 2020s by the Microslices model of tightly packaged, niche delivery that is often automated. At first, several large firms maintained—almost insisted—that the new model was impure or a fad and focused their attention on organizations that were technological laggards or whose corporate cultures rejected innovation or technology adoption. They strictly adhered to the "trusted advisor" model of the 20th century, which, to be fair, was exactly what their largest clients wanted. Now those last few clients either have newer executives who reject the old model outright or have disappeared to more innovative competitors themselves.

Some will reject this notion. By the time they figure out what's going on, it's going to be too late. Their competitors, who *do* take advantage of Microslicing and change the way they buy consulting and professional services, are going to be too far ahead to catch. The laggards will sit in their nice leather chairs in their high-end consultancy's 50th floor office, admiring the commissioned art, and feel safe. But they won't be.

Intentionally Adopting a Millennial Attitude

As reluctant as I am to give away any more secrets, I'll share one more piece of inside baseball. In my company, we are aggressively and intentionally adopting millennial culture. We're constantly trying out new ideas, new approaches, and new technology. Instead of buying bigger tech as we've grown, we have gone smaller to "lightweight" tech products that work with open APIs. Beyond our toolkit, we allow our millennial thinkers to drive our social interactions, take charge of important projects, and even design our company hoodies.

We don't do that to manage projects and deliver results; we do it to prepare ourselves for the future. Instead of worrying about people's qualifications on data science, we pay them to take courses while compensating them for the work that they do. Starting with myself and going all the way down to people who might not have a millennial attitude even if they're young, we are actively trying to change our company's attitudes.

The technology is certainly part of it, but that's just one instrument of change. Insistence on learning is part of it, too, even as it applies to how we think about results. I mentioned before that people who are millennials tend to want results, and they want them now. A lot of our clients, believe it or not, are not terribly interested in the detailed calculation of results for the work that we're doing with them. We find this strange, so we do it anyway.

We're developing internal methodologies that enable us to quickly calculate value for our clients, even if they don't request it. And even when they don't request it or want it, we calculate it internally, so that we know the answer, allowing us to keep track of our own data and make internal improvements in our delivery. As a company that has adopted a millennial attitude and is building its culture around that concept, it's critical that, internally, we have an understanding of the value we're delivering.

BIG SKY'S RESULTS MANIFESTO

1. *Time and value are not equivalent.* We will provide maximum value in as little time as possible. The old model of charging on the basis of time is broken. We will never take longer than necessary to deliver a result.

2. *Work is something you do, not a place you go.*[41] Our work culture rejects "presentee-ism" (a belief system based on people being physically present) in favor of presenting killer results.

3. *Do unto ourselves as we would have our clients do unto us.* Big Sky's relationship with its employees should mirror our relationship with our clients. In other words, we

41 | Cali Ressler and Jody Thompson. *Why Work Sucks and How to Fix It: The Results-Only Revolution.* Portfolio, 2010.

expect our clients to respect us and focus on results, so we should do the same to each other.

4. *Greatness isn't for everyone.* Some executives really want to pay to see someone sitting in a cube at their facility, no matter how good or bad the work is. Some executives really want to pay to direct the details of how the work is done instead of for a specific result, which requires them to be charged by the hour. We believe that we should prove that our way is better—but that requires clients who accept proof.

Before we move into part II of this book, I'd like to recap what we've learned so far:

In chapter 1, we took an eagle's view of Microslices. In chapter 2, we articulated growth and looked at how data science is driving the move toward Microslices through innovative and sophisticated interpretation of data. Chapter 3 touched on three crucial and rapidly accelerating technologies that make those slices available, accessible, and insightful. Finally, in this chapter we presented the cultural shift that's taking place and that allows Microslices to stick.

Part II of this book puts these concepts to work by explaining what the Microslices future looks like and what you must do about it.

CHAPTER 4 SUMMARY

○ Widespread adoption—in society at large as well as in your organization—of a "millennial attitude" is the third critical enabler of Microslices.

○ A millennial attitude isn't about a specific generation—it is a set of beliefs and preferences that change the way executives will buy professional services.

○ The first ingredient in a millennial attitude is a high level of trust in technology, coupled with relatively low trust in people.

○ The second ingredient in a millennial attitude is a results orientation—a focus on outcomes rather than a focus on activity.

○ The third ingredient in a millennial attitude is a willingness to experiment, which manifests itself as limited loyalty to traditional methods, processes, and technologies.

○ Millennial attitudes will become the norm in your organization's C-suite in just a few years, especially as these attitudes become prevalent beyond the post-1980 generation.

○ This change will cause more rapid adoption of the technology and data science described in previous chapters and will accelerate the impact on professional services.

○ Firms that believe that only data science and technology are important are at very high risk of failure; the cultural change required is equally disruptive and important.

○ As an executive who buys professional services, your charge is to take action to drive adoption of a millennial attitude in your organization.

MICROSLICES
IN ACTION

CHAPTER 5

A HISTORY OF FUTURE ADVICE

The future ain't what it used to be.

–Yogi Berra

et's pretend we're in 2030. The emergence of Microslices is as obvious to me as the history of the Internet is to you, largely because of the developments in technology, data science, and knowledge worker culture.

We focus here on the 15 years from 2015 to 2030, because that's the time frame that many organizations—government and commercial—made decisions and began to change what they did. The future, quite frankly, is very unpredictable after 2030—we simply don't know how fast things are going to progress.

2015—A Tipping Point

If you're reading this book, you're probably reading it in 2015 or 2016. If you're reading it after that, it's probably outdated—that's how fast things are changing. The following are some key events in 2015 that heralded the beginning of Microslices and how they occurred.

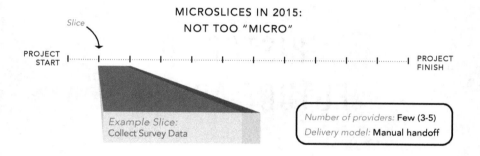

The first one: a boardroom version of IBM's media darling and Jeopardy winner, Watson, completed a world tour to show off its business acumen and its ability to answer questions other than word puzzles. Watson was demonstrated at companies all over the world to answer questions like: "Which company should we acquire to advance our AI strategy?" and "Which executives consistently provide the best input at board meetings?"

Looking back at 2015, Watson was a resounding success. It attracted a lot of attention, despite the fact that it wasn't that good at natural language and made a few mistakes. Nonetheless, Watson was a promising development.[42]

42 | Tim Simonite, "A Room Where Executives Go to Get Help from IBM's Watson," August 4, 2014, http://www.technologyreview.com/news/529606/a-room-where-executives-go-to-get-help-from-ibms-watson/

Also that year, gamers rejoiced when "affective computing," which uses sensors such as infrared, breath analysis, and temperature detection, allowed games to dynamically react to the emotions of the gamer.[43]

The oldest millennials turned 35 and started appearing in C-suites of the Fortune 500. Some stock traders already used a form of artificial intelligence to place orders in milliseconds. Knowing this, CNBC and Singularity University hosted a conference on "Quantum Finance" in December 2015 where speakers proved that quantum computing outperform classical options pricing models, breaking a barrier to commercial use of the technology.[44]

In 2015, the world produced eight zettabytes of data. If you're wondering, that's about 8,000 exabytes, which is 8 *trillion* gigabytes—a number that most human brains in 2015 can't comprehend. *That figure represents 700 times the estimated information content of all human knowledge in 1999.*

By the end of 2015, the data science specialization was ten times more popular than every other existing certification on Coursera. Statisticians everywhere were angered that someone came along and made their job cool.

43 | Nick Bilton, "Devices That Know How We Really Feel," May 4, 2014, http://bits. blogs.nytimes.com/2014/05/04/devices-that-know-how-we-really-feel/

44 | "Advances in big data analysis may change the way analysts do their job, augmenting or replacing spreadsheets with intelligent analytics software that can harvest key insights from the daily deluge of financial and economic data or keep a watchful eye on consumer behavior and activity to prevent fraud."

Source: Singularity University, "Discover the Convergence of Tech and Finance at the Exponential Finance Conference, June 10-11," May 9, 2014. http://singularityhub. com/2014/05/09/discover-the-convergence-of-tech-and-finance-at-the-exponential-finance-conference-june-10-11/

It was a great year, 2015. It got the ball rolling—it's the first year I can look back to from my perch in 2030 and say that Microslices was really getting some traction in professional services.

While impressive, those Microslices were not very "micro" back in 2015, as you can see from the chart. They were really just apps, like , HR functions like Yoi, and custom models for specific kinds of scenarios, like pricing models and demand analyses.

There were companies in 2015 that built custom models for different kinds of scenarios, like pricing analysis, demand analysis, and risk analysis. But those modules were still fairly big and broad. Those companies began to sell Microslices and package them as products. But still, the dominant model by far remained traditional time- and materials-based consulting. But the upstarts were making progress.

2020—Bigger Data, Smaller Slices

Moore's Law was still going strong in 2020, meaning technological advancement was growing at an exponential rate and had a huge effect on how services were delivered. The total information in the world reached 40 zettabytes.

By 2020, practically everyone on earth walked around with some sort of sensor or cell phone in their hand or embedded in their clothing (and, for a few, embedded in their bodies[45]). Jobs in data science were so much in demand that innovative educational

45 | I know this sounds creepy, but in truth, embedded sensors have been around for some time, most commonly in cardiac patients who have defibrillators implanted in their chests that transmit data to doctors on a daily basis.

institutions sprung up to meet the demand—while traditional educational institutions, their offerings dated, began to spiral into financial distress. The two disciplines of computer science and data science continued to merge into one unified approach to solving information problems. Data scientists couldn't do it alone, and computer scientists who didn't understand statistics struggled to get a job.

AI progress remained somewhat disappointing and brute-force oriented. It did get better at processing all of the sensors and data, but it was still pretty bad at deriving meaning from context and data. Netflix continued to insist that customers who watched *Pride and Prejudice* should be interested in *Nanny McPhee*.

MICROSLICES IN 2020

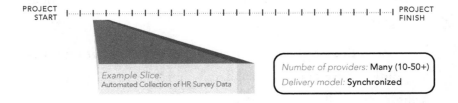

PROJECT START | PROJECT FINISH

Example Slice:
Automated Collection of HR Survey Data

Number of providers: **Many (10-50+)**
Delivery model: **Synchronized**

By 2020, Microslices really began to show its promise. Specialized firms that offered specialized products (still wrapped in some traditional consulting services) far outpaced the growth of traditional firms. Companies that used unstructured data analysis (like free text mining) saw their margins balloon and their advice improve dramatically. Hourly billing began to retreat to large, calcified industries like government where contracting was slow to change and adapt. In turn, the gap between those companies that hired Microslicing consultants and those that continued to hire traditional consultants widened. The companies that hired Microslicing firms showed demonstrably better results.

This pattern was mirrored in the legal, accounting, and medical professions as regulatory structures became ever more complex and arcane in these fields. In short, computers and automation were absolutely required to make sense of the insanity of bureaucratic regulation. Humans doing legal, accounting, and medical jobs began to specialize in things that still only humans could do. But that list got shorter.

By 2020, core analytical processes like hypothesis tests, root-cause analysis, acquisition selection, and project portfolio analysis became a part of the Microslicing phenomenon, building on the more mundane and repeatable tasks that were Microsliced in 2015. In other words, by 2020 you didn't need a human to determine what the root causes of your problem were. You could use a computer to do it for you.

Consulting firms, whose profits were driven by large numbers of hourly consultants, consolidated rapidly. Small, tech-savvy firms grew rapidly without acquisition.

At the same time, millennial CEOs and executives emerged as a different kind of consulting buyer. These new leaders started to employ the first AI-assisted corporate decision-making technologies, which caused regulators and business ethicists to openly debate the societal and cultural consequences of AI-driven strategy in corporate firms.

2030—Clarke's Third Law

*Any sufficiently advanced technology is
indistinguishable from magic.*

—Arthur C. Clarke

In 2030, not just in consulting but in knowledge work in general,
things get weird.[46] The knowledge worker segment of the economy,
including professional services, is quite frankly indistinguishable
from what you know in 2015.

MICROSLICES IN 2030

PROJECT START · PROJECT FINISH

Example Slice:
Background Analysis of Employee Behavior
Suggests Conclusions Before You Ask

Number of providers:
n (countless)

Delivery model:
**Seemless and
imperceptible**

Contrary to the warnings of authors like Jaron Lanier in
2015, humans are not losing their jobs permanently. But there
has definitely been a lot of displacement. We are still figuring out

---

46 | **Clarke's Three Laws** are three "laws" of prediction formulated by the British science
fiction writer Arthur C. Clarke: (1) When a distinguished but elderly scientist states that
something is possible, he is almost certainly right. When he states that something is
impossible, he is very probably wrong. (2) The only way of discovering the limits of
the possible is to venture a little way past them into the impossible. (3) Any sufficiently
advanced technology is indistinguishable from magic.

Source: "Clarke's three laws," Wikipedia. http://en.m.wikipedia.org/wiki/
Clarke%27s_three_laws

how to properly compensate people for their intellectual property and their knowledge because data is so dispersed. On the flip side, there are countless new jobs and new services that have sprung up to provide functions that folks in 2015 haven't even thought of yet. To the surprise of many, opportunity for strong wages, fulfilling work, innovation, and discovery has grown, pulling ever more millions out of poverty, especially in less developed nations.

In 2030, sensors and AI are ubiquitous—it is in our clothing, our furniture, our buildings, and, most recently, within our bodies. At least one trillion sensors are measuring the information in the physical world. That translates to about 150 sensors to every person on earth.[47] Keep in mind, the population is still exploding.

"Zettabyte" was a unit of measure most people didn't even know in 2015, and we don't use it much anymore—it's too small. Artificial intelligence isn't quite what 2015 movies made it out to be. However, machines have proven to be both capable and creative. They pass every version of the Turing test we can concoct for them.[48] In digital environments, they're often indistinguishable from humans in their communication skills. In short, sometimes I don't even know whether I'm talking to a computer or a consultant. Most of us are okay with that—it's the new normal.

---

47 | "Information Optimization: Harness the power of big data," http://h41145. www4.hp.com/events/discover/frankfurt/pdfs/IO_PoV_Whitepaper_Harness_the_ Power_of_Big_Data.pdf

48 | "The **Turing test** is a test of a machine's ability to exhibit intelligent behavior equivalent to, or indistinguishable from, that of a human."

Source: "Turing test," Wikipedia. en.wikipedia.org/wiki/Turing_test

Many have benefited from the incredible developments in health science and information technology, and most people rapidly adopt to artificial enhancements—such as bionic limbs and sensory implants—and how we use them in order to achieve goals that are good for humanity. Access to the latest and most expensive health technology reaches the wealthiest first, but that does little to diminish the remarkable gains available to the *poorest* on earth, whose lifespans have increased (by percentage) faster than any other demographic group since 2020.

Distance and time of day are increasingly unimportant. On consulting engagements, businesses and governments that have problems simply want them solved. Our attitude toward solving those problems doesn't just *allow* us to trust computers to help us, it requires that we trust computers to help us.

But it's not all rosy: 2020 to 2025 was a crisis period for employment and intellectual property law—the old regulatory and legal structures that we used for the economy stopped making sense. Ownership of information has become very challenging to manage, partly because solutions to problems are produced by both intelligent machines and humans working together. Important legal constructs on child labor law, ownership of information, intellectual property rights, "personhood," and health and safety law turned upside down between 2025 and 2030.

Even now in 2030, consultants and advisors who consult companies on how to deploy technology that enabled Microslices have themselves been replaced by advice-giving technology.

Advanced AI is not only helping us solve problems that used to be solved by traditional consulting; technology is *advising* us on how to deploy *more* advanced technology. Mutually reinforcing technology allows mutually reinforcing innovations in service delivery. Faster hardware has allowed us to design better algorithms, which has allowed us to build faster hardware. That same "virtuous cycle" has accelerated the development of new and different business models for deploying expertise and knowledge.

VIRTUOUS CYCLE

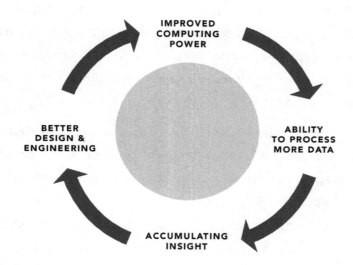

By 2030, the Microslices model is the prevailing delivery model for giving and receiving advice.

As Arthur C. Clarke would have put it, Microslices—the specialization, automation, and compression of consulting activities—has become almost like *magic*. It's just something that—while incredibly complex behind the curtain—is simply the way things work.

Specialization

As shown in the graphic above, slices aren't just small. They are getting smaller every day in 2030. Because so much data is available and produced and connected by open APIs, solutions are becoming incredibly specialized.

For example: A single project or problem is solved by thousands of connected slices of code and expertise owned by many individuals and companies. (Not by just one consultant.) Those slices are so specialized that they focus not on a problem like improving loan forecasts in general but instead focus on one tenth of that forecast, tailored to your company's geography and exact size and customer base.

Automation

Automation in 2030 means that almost all of these Microslices are delivered automatically without much human intervention. Sometimes, an executive or a government leader simply asks his or her advisory interface (think Siri or Google Now), "How do we improve our loan processes?" or "What are the lowest costs and ways to improve our security by 20 percent?" The answers still aren't 100 percent, but they allow executives to focus on the very few things that matter most.

That advisory interface instantly kludges thousands of network solution providers, algorithms, and data to provide you the answer in whatever format is required. That might be synthetic speech. It might be a presentation. It might be a written document.

What's more, the AI in your advisory interface is inventing new Microslices on its own without human intervention. That means it operates independently to predict and develop potential solutions for as yet unidentified problems and queues those up for you as possible questions to ask. So instead of asking your computer for help, it may reach out to you and say, "Hey, would you like to know how to decrease your capital costs by 12 percent without sacrificing quality?" And you can answer, "Sure…that would be great."

Compression

In 2015, consultants would often do things that may or may not have been necessary because they weren't sure what they would need to do. The automation in Microslicing allows us to eliminate those extraneous steps and shorten the time frame of delivery.

Furthermore, all the processing power and networks allow even highly complex, dynamic problems to be analyzed and solved quickly. If data is already available in the problem, solutions that used to take months take minutes, including recommended implementation steps.

Often, the automation extends to launching those implementation steps. Only physical data collection, meaning deploying new sensors to a new place where there are no sensors today, slows things down. That's pretty rare, since sensors are nearly everywhere, on everyone, all the time. Don't forget that in 2030 there are about 150 sensors for every human on earth. It can still take a few hours for drones to deploy sensors in remote locations, and space launches are still an expensive headache, but otherwise, things happen fast.

Putting all of this together, the process by which even the simplest advice is given—such as "How does franchise law affect our expansion plans?" involves thousands of specialized machines and individuals, organized within minutes, drawing from billions of data points. As this networked delivery model is too complex to be assembled by human advice givers, machines help us identify, connect with, translate, organize, summarize, and otherwise construct the network of delivery required to deal with most organizational advice problems. Furthermore, those dynamic networks of delivery models anticipate additional problems and challenges.

In 2015 the US Department of Defense found it very difficult to account for all of its assets, which affected everything from accounting to locating resources (especially small, inexpensive materials and equipment). In 2030 the DoD can calculate the location, status, and value of all of its assets and can have an up-to-date audit nearly instantly. In fact, everywhere on earth, all pieces of military equipment, all military employees, and all civilians in military carry at least a dozen sensors each, if only to communicate location. As such, the US Secretary of Defense can simply ask, "What is the approximate asset value of everything that the department owns?" and the computer will simply tell her.

In a practical example related to reallocating defense resources, in 2029 the Chairman of the Senate Armed Services Committee wanted to find a way to divest assets to raise money for a new weapons system. Since he has access to all of DoD's data and public data sets from his "automated advisor," he simply asked. That advisor recommended that he sell thousands of acres of beachfront DoD property all over the world that was sparsely populated and didn't hold much strategic value. Not long thereafter, they raised 1 trillion 2029 dollars, which they were able to reallocate to justify the new weapons system.

YOU, THE EXECUTIVE, MUST ACT

They claimed that too many things could never be commoditized in consulting. Why try something new, they asked, when what they've been doing has worked so well for so long? We are familiar with these objections—and not at all swayed by them. If our long study of disruption has led us to any universal conclusion, it is that every industry will eventually face it.

—Clayton Christensen

What does this glimpse of the future mean for you? First, let's review the ideas we've covered so far.

1. Data science, certain technologies, and millennial culture are disrupting the professional services industry in dramatic and unexpected ways.

2. Change is afoot and will accelerate over the next 15 years until the model for how you hire consultants—

as well as accountants, lawyers, and other professional services providers—will have radically changed.

3.   The dominant model that will emerge is Microslices—the accelerating compression, specialization, and automation of professional services.

That's where the new face of professional services comes in. This is not a story of the future. This is what you can do right now.

Only You (the Client) Can Break Up the Traditional Professional Services Cult

We now know that real changes are in store for both you and the professional services you buy. Fifteen years is not a long time. There's a lot happening around you right now. It's time to act.

As we mentioned earlier, consultants, lawyers, accountants, and doctors have been aware of these trends and opportunities but add a little incentive to act on them. Automation, compression, and specialization of our advice—and the demise of the hourly-rate project—is often not in the traditional firm or practice's interest.

Christiensen's Four Trends to Watch in Consulting[49]

O   Thinning the ranks of top firms—a consolidation that will topple some top firms but strengthen others.

O   Smaller clients will lead the way while the traditional press will obsess over industry leaders with big clients; smaller clients with niche challenges will be the first to adapt.

---

49 | Clayton Christensen. *The Innovator's Dilemma: When New Technologies Cause Great Firms to Fail (Management of Innovation and Change).* Harvard Business Review Press; 1997.

- Blurred lines—the distinctions between professional services firms will blur, creating overlaps and opportunities between law, consulting, accounting, and even medicine.

- Invasion of hard analytics—hard analytics and technology (big data) will reshape not just delivery work but the method of delivery itself.

For 20 years, professional services firms have not adapted technology in many cases, and no one has called them out on it. Why are we still billing by the hour? Why do we still use a 20-year-old model? Who is to blame? The client. But the client can also be the solution.

Here's why: The reality is that the client allows hourly billing and many of the other bad habits presented in this book. The client is the one who worries about when the consultant is actually working when it doesn't really matter for the task at hand. The client doesn't often insist that a specific measurable result be obtained when they hire professional services.

The bottom line is that as a client of professional services, you don't want to pay for outdated practices, technological or data science illiteracy, or rigid delivery models. And you shouldn't. In most cases, companies are going to sell what buyers will buy. If change is to occur, it's you who will ultimately drive it.

Throughout this book, I've made the case that over the course of the next 15 years, it's very likely that the information in your company will expand and become more accessible. With advances described in this book, you'll soon ask your AI assistant for a way to cut your costs by 20 percent and get a helpful, if not perfect, answer. This new capability is going to put a lot of consultants out of business. If you're not planning ahead, it might put you out of business, too. If you're a government leader or a nonprofit, it might cause you to fail at your core mission, whether that's delivering services to the needy or being able to deploy forces to a far-flung region of the earth. The good news is that you have an opportunity to take advantage of this change to choose the advisors you rely on...and to choose them wisely.

There are specific, tangible steps you can take right now to change the way you find, hire, and manage—and sometimes dismiss—your advisors. These steps allow you to make choices based on how much you value the results those firms will provide, instead of the good feeling that they gave you in a meeting. We'll go through these steps in chapter 7.

When it comes down to successfully selecting and using professional services firms, the ball is in your court. You have options, and you must intentionally exercise them. They're not going to happen by themselves.

5 Irrational Objections to Microslices

- ○ "Get those kids off of my lawn!" (The millennial objection)

- ○ "If it ain't broke don't fix it." (The steady-as-she-goes objection)

- ○ "I need someone I can trust." (The whites-of-their-eyes objection)

- ○ "Nobody ever got fired for hiring [insert top brand here]." (The Rolex watch objection)

○ "There's no way a computer will ever be able to do this."
(The there-will-always-be-newspapers objection)

These objections to Microslices don't hold water.

The Millennial Objection

Like every generation before them, millennials are accused of being demanding, overindulged, and entitled. They want feedback all the time. They insist on instant gratification, and they all got trophies growing up no matter how badly they played soccer.

While generalizing about generational differences is a national pastime, it would be a mistake for an executive to confuse the trends I've described in part I with generational preferences. If you are skeptical of automation, compression, and specialization because you believe that it's just a fad among the 20–35-year-old set, you will miss opportunities that your competitors will exploit.

The Steady-as-She-Goes Objection

Business books are filled with companies and governments that "prepared for the last war" by sticking blindly to processes and methods that work today. If you've been paying attention to the last 50 years, that's not a great way to operate. In every industry, eventually technology and innovation force change. In professional services, that change will be coming fast, and the cost of failing to anticipate may be crippling.

The Whites-of-Their-Eyes Objection

For many of us, the idea of accepting advice from a person on the other side of the country or even from a computer challenges our notions of trust and accountability. You might feel that you need someone who can look you in the eye and shake your hand. Unfortunately, this gut-feel approach can lead to poorer decision making. As we all know, a person can look right at you and lie, exaggerate, or obfuscate. Personal connections are important in many aspects of our lives, but technology can reliably reproduce those connections and even enhance them. Continuing to rely on the professional sitting in a cubicle down the hall won't end well.

The Rolex Watch Objection

You might have heard the expression "nobody ever got fired for hiring IBM" (or perhaps you heard it with McKinsey, Microsoft, or another esteemed brand instead of IBM). As Microslices becomes the dominant model for consulting and results are more transparent to the buyer, many consulting services will become commoditized and automated. In some cases, those great brands will stay great by delivering great results. However, if you need to tell the time and that is your purpose, you do not need a Rolex watch. You may want one, but if you need to know what time it is, it is not necessary.

The There-Will-Always-Be-Newspapers Objection

There is, and always has been, a segment of society that insists that a computer can't do something a human can, and then, sure enough, a computer does it. Let's face it: leaders need advice, and there is great honor in providing it. But as an executive, you must be prepared to change the way that you buy that advice. You need solutions to increasingly complex problems—and you need them faster than ever, because your competitors are adapting. The only way to go faster for less money is to embrace the automation of many of the functions your professional services provide today. Just as it's foolish to adopt technology for technology's sake, it's foolish to ignore technology when it delivers the result you need.

But I've been using the same firm for twenty years...

As you've read this book, you may have begun to question the value of the firms with which you've done—or are doing—business. In fact, you might even be a little angry at them now that you realize that there are better models that tip things in your favor, both financially and in the value of the advice you receive. It's okay to feel that way. This is a process, not a quick fix. The vast majority of consultants have their clients' best interests at heart, so I would ask you to temper that anger a little. If your professional services partners are changing—and some are—you will have the pleasure of entering this new era with them. There may be fewer of them, and they may have different skills, but some firms are taking steps to make the change. You may be able to preserve some long-standing relationships, and I hope that you can. The following chapters will help you discern whether that's possible.

Time to Put Your Cards on the Table

You do in fact need to ask yourself some critical questions before you read the next chapter on finding the right firm.

○ Do you know how your professional service providers deliver today?

○ Are your professional service providers open to new ways of working together, and are you?

○ Do you keep a services team? How much are you paying? How much value do you receive? Do you have a good understanding of what that even means?

○ Do you and your service providers discuss how to use technology to improve delivery and results?

○ Can you accept that you don't always have to see someone to trust that the work is being done?

○ Are you willing and able to accept that the advice you are getting isn't always going to be from a human being?

Indulge me for a moment while I conduct a thought experiment.

1. Think of the three smartest, most capable, and talented people on your team. Keep in mind how their performance is evaluated by your organization.

2. Envision a problem, preferably a real one, with specific results that you want to achieve, such as a solution to a complex operations problem.

3. Imagine that you have instructed each of them to solve the problem separately, without communication or further instruction, and when they are finished to stop working altogether until one month has passed.

The first employee, Susan, solves it in a shocking four minutes, giving the perfect answer. She expended almost no effort whatsoever, and you have no knowledge of how she got it done. She spends the remainder of the month learning how to play the guitar, reconnecting with her long-lost sister, and working in an animal rescue center.

Tom solves it in a respectable four days, also giving the perfect answer. As with Susan, you have no knowledge of how he got it done. He spends the remainder of the month training for the US National Biathlon team and binge-watching *House of Cards*.

Nelson solves it in four weeks, also giving the perfect answer. As with Susan and Tom, you don't know how he did it. With no remaining time available, he enthusiastically delivers your requested answer and gets ready for next week.

Question 1: You are required to provide the best performer with a $1,000 bonus, based exclusively on the performance criteria set out by your organization in #3 above. Who gets the bonus?

Question 2: Imagine that each of the people above is a consultant and you are required to pay each a fair fee. How much do you pay each?

Your answer to the questions above might provoke a lot of tough thinking. Perhaps you're wondering what the hell took Nelson so long. Maybe you realized that your performance evaluation criteria don't make much sense. Alternatively, you're struggling to make a decision at all because all three did exactly as they were asked. Maybe you're thinking that Susan tricked you out of $1,000 or that Nelson worked the hardest.

It is clear, however, which result was objectively best for the organization: Susan's. Time is money, and you got the result sooner.

Just as clear, however, is that in the hourly-rate model for professional services, Nelson would earn the most money for solving the problem. That doesn't make sense, does it?

Microslices will make it easier for you to break free from the tyranny of the labor hour as a measure of value. Why not pay Susan the most money and put them onto solving a second, third, and fourth problem? There should be huge incentives on both sides in that.

The outline I've presented of the Microslices model only scratches the surface of what it is and what it means. To fully understand how you can put Microslices to work in your organization, you need to understand its characteristics and how those differ from traditional professional services.

We have discussed the Microslices business model, which describes how consulting would work. It doesn't describe some of the principles around that model.

Below are seven core principles surrounding the Microslices model that every executive needs to understand. These principles will be critical as you work through the next chapter on the specific steps you can take to adapt.

7 CORE PRINCIPLES

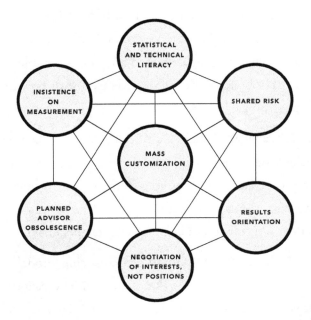

1. **Statistical and technical literacy.** First and foremost, Microslicing requires an understanding of the interaction of data science and technology.

2. **Shared risk.** Microslicing requires service providers and buyers to have a stake in the outcome and to act in good faith to achieve it. That means that consulting providers might be willing to put their fees at stake. Gamesmanship, deception, and unethical behavior are deal breakers.

3. **Results orientation.** As more consulting functions are replaced by automation, a premium should be placed on the (measurable) outcome—not the process or effort required to produce it. Executives that hire firms that utilize Microslices will be freed from the tyranny of the labor hour and can focus on measurable value.

4. **Negotiation of interests, not positions.** This is not my idea; it is straight out of a classic negotiation book called *Getting to Yes*[50]. As a project and fees are negotiated, it's crucial that parties focus on what is to be delivered and the timetable, not on the details of how the work is going to be done or how many hours are spent on each step.

5. **Planned advisor obsolescence.** Microslices, as they become smaller, more automated, and more culturally accepted, are going to be easily transferrable from advisor to buyer. The goal of advisors should therefore be to *replace themselves*. That's what my firm is trying to do: help our clients operate after we're gone.

6. **Insistence on measurement.** Microslicing models just won't work if it's not clear how value is created. Microslices is a model that will make measurement easier and make measurement the basis for demonstrating value. As solutions get more complex, involving a network of firms and individuals, each node of that network must be able to measure and share data quickly and automatically. The bottom line is that everything must be measured, even intangibles like morale, fit, and alignment— things that you used to just trust to good judgment and gut feel.

7. **Mass customization.** This 2000s-era manufacturing term needs to be resuscitated for the emergence of Microslices in professional services. In the context of professional services, it implies that a broad scope of modular, specialized advisory "components" can be assembled quickly to create a completely customized professional services solution for a client. The Microslicing model requires adaptation in order to rapidly

50 | Roger Fisher and William Ury. *Getting to Yes: Negotiating Agreement without Giving In*. New York: Penguin, 2011.

deploy and tightly customize methods, solutions, and results for every client. This means there can be no more "cookie cutter" solutions, even for large-scale automated processes.

ATTENTION: GOVERNMENT READERS

Microslices Isn't Just Happening in the Private Sector—It's Changing Government

If you're a government leader, you might be thinking that there are some interesting points in this book but that government is different. Good news: you're right! The government is different because it spends a hell of a lot more on professional services than any other entity in the world. The US federal government alone spent $308 billion on services contracts in 2012.51 That's roughly equivalent to the nominal GDP of Denmark.

There are clear signs that the fundamental nature of the consulting and contracting business is changing for the government. First, organizations like CSIS are reporting that the government is becoming more dependent on services contractors, not less. Second, spending on services is actually shrinking and seems to be hitting the biggest firms the hardest. Third, the government is investing in massive data and technology infrastructure projects to take advantage of trends we've outlined in this book. Acquisition reform is beginning to get legs, as evidenced by new vehicles and methods being advanced by GSA, the Air Force, and unique entities like 18F.

This change is in fact the beginning of the disruptive innovation that will foment the Microslices model for government. As

51 | Marjorie Censer, "Signs point to rockier road for services contractors," *Washington Post*, September 10 2013.

we've explained, consulting and contracting will compress (shorter timelines), specialize (more niche players), and automate (services delivered by machines or technology). In many ways, the government is most susceptible to Microslicing. Let's revisit the frameworks I introduced above, from the perspective of the government buyer.

Earlier in this chapter, I referenced four near-term implications of disruptive innovation in consulting. Below is a chart showing how each of those four implications are playing out in the government.

Near-term trend	Possible early signs	What it means for government
A consolidation—a thinning of the ranks—in the top tiers of the industry	Top contractors like SAIC and Deloitte cite price pressure and shrinking revenue and profit. L-3, SAIC, and CIBER spin off federal services divisions. Scitor purchased in 2015 by SAIC for $790 million.	Government pressure to reduce hourly fees will result in consolidation among large, staff-heavy contractors, along with a degradation of quality in traditional service models.
Change begins with smaller clients served by niche players	Despite the drumbeat of news on sequestration and the 2016 budget, 18F, GSA, and the Air Force pioneer agile and lean procurement, focusing on open source solutions and APIs, many of which solve problems by automating the analysis of data sets.	Industry associations like AFCEA and the press focus on big programs and big contracts, but small agencies will hire small firms to do things very differently—and will get more for less.
Blurring of traditional professional services boundaries	Palantir, which focuses on automated analysis, was founded in 2004 and is now worth $9 billion. Meanwhile, traditional services contractors report shrinking federal revenue and profit. Small analytics firms are getting traction doing the work of SETA contractors using algorithms.	Defense tech firms that have performed systems integration work or staffing will see margins shrink, forcing them into new markets (including commercial), and products companies with unique offerings (like AI and analytics firms) will cross over into what traditionally has been solved by contractors or consultants.
Invasion of hard analytics (big data)	Traditional government functions like personnel management, security, and policy analysis are investing heavily in hard analytics to solve the problems previously solved by specialists. One DoD command is testing advanced analytics to "read" RFPs and proposals to better analyze them. No government function will be untouched by analytics within 15 years.	The government is spending untold billions (untold because it's classified) on analytics and big data—they are more than likely the largest spender on big data in the world and always have been. No organization stands to gain more from AI and hard analytics than the US government.

If you agree that Microslices is real for government, the next question is what to do about it given the peculiarities of government contracting. Government contracts are much bigger, are subject to far more scrutiny, and are saddled with incredibly voluminous rules and regulations and in many ways are designed to protect the status quo.

Unfortunately for the government executive, the acquisition system is not conducive to buying Microslices. As government executives know, contracts are usually large and long term because they are so incredibly hard to set up. They are notoriously inflexible once they are set up. Do the math: if it takes hundreds of person-hours to set up a $10,000 contract, why would you bother? However, it can be done if the executive is committed and the contracting officer is resourceful.

The need for acquisition reform is even more critical in light of the advance of Microslices in professional services. The government's failure to reform acquisition to adapt to these trends will have serious negative consequences for the American public, the provision of basic government services, and the defense and security of the country.

As a government official, a failure to adapt means that you may waste resources, slip into embarrassingly poor performance, or worse, end up on the front page of the Washington Post. That embarrassment might be a public disclosure, the failure to detect or mitigate a security threat, or the failure to provide basic support services like medical care or safety net benefits.

Five Pro Tips for Contracting for Microslices

1. *Find a resourceful contracting officer (CO).* Without someone who is smart, committed, and ethical, you won't get anywhere. That person may be outside of your

organization. They are easy to identify: they don't start conversations by saying no.

2. *Buy faster by using programs like 8(a) and HUBZone.* Not because they are a noble cause but because they provide COs far more flexibility and speed than traditional methods.

3. *Use simplified acquisition procedures.* Most people don't know that there is a completely different set of contracting rules for small purchases. What's more, when coupled with tip #2, those rules can be applied to many more procurements.

4. *Don't ask general counsel for permission.* They're good people, really. But they are heavily incentivized to insulate you from new ideas. COs know the law and ethical standards and are more than capable of staying within the law, so stick with them unless they tell you to call the lawyers.

5. *Don't give up.* It's easy to get frustrated, but sometimes it's just a matter of looking at the problem from a different angle or asking for another expert perspective.

Government Officials: Adapt to Microslices or Embrace Failure

Earlier in this chapter, I outlined seven core principles that every executive needs to understand in order to adapt to Microslices. This will be more difficult for the federal executive but even more important given the massive spending on services and the reality that change will not slow down for the public sector. In fact, Microslices—more than cost overruns, fraud, waste, or abuse—is *the* burning platform for acquisition reform. If you are a federal executive and apply these core principles, you will outpace your peers, achieve greater results, and help shepherd in a new era of excellence in government service.

1. **Statistical and technical literacy.** This must be required for every contractor. These skills are even less prevalent in the government, outside of selected pockets of excellence.

2. **Shared risk.** In my years of experience in the federal government, I have seen a remarkable lack of understanding of how to share risk with consultants and contractors. While allowable in the Federal Acquisition Regulations (FAR), contracting officers avoid risk sharing because it is not the norm, and they are trained to conflate innovation with risk. For the government to avoid dangerous mismanagement in the Microslices era, it *must* learn to build contracts that share risk with consultants using fixed and value pricing.

3. **Results orientation.** The government often mistakenly links costs expended or hours worked with value. This "tyranny of the labor hour" is unequivocally wrongheaded and must change, especially for contractors and consultants. At Big Sky, whether our clients want it or not, we calculate the value delivered (in dollars wherever possible) on every single engagement. Excluding only truly exceptional circumstances, you should not work with a contractor or consultant again **unless the price is based on the results delivered.** For example, $5 million might seem like a lot of money for a yearlong project to fix an administrative process. However, if the *impact* of that project is $75

million, after all costs, then it's a bargain. If you don't know what the results are and can't measure those results, don't cut the contract.

4.   **Negotiation of interests, not positions.** The idea of negotiating based on interests, not positions, was (surprisingly) pioneered by the government itself—in international treaty negotiation. Nonetheless, contracting officers and government executives—and contractors—doggedly cling to rigid positions on hourly or cost-plus billing or antiquated reporting rules. Instead, government agencies should focus on their interests: the *results* they need, instead of taking "positions" in an RFP or procurement that box the agency into a corner (and an inferior result).

5.   **Planned advisor obsolescence.** As evidenced in the CSIS research cited earlier in this chapter, the government is becoming more dependent on outside consultants and contractors to perform basic work. What better way to break free of that dependency than to embrace Microslices—which by definition are small, automated, and transferrable services capabilities?

6.   **Insistence on measurement.** Measurement is a dirty word with many of my company's government clients, not because they don't want to measure but because they *fear to report* those measures. For example, it's fairly easy to calculate cost savings from a process improvement—but reporting those savings could mean a reduction in the organization's budget! As a result, government executives avoid routine, precise measurement because

the wrong number could be "bureaucratically incorrect." In other words, *lack of knowledge is preferable to bad news.* It's crucial that government executives, while managing bureaucratic realities, find a way to measure and to use measurement to make better choices.

7. **Mass customization.** The government no longer needs to return, over and over again, to a handful of massive contractors. Those big companies often do great work, but government executives need diverse and innovative ideas from a variety of sources. Analytics, computing power, and networked service delivery allow for the power of a large firm delivered with a team of small, specialized ones. There are places for big players, but government leaders should recognize that the networked delivery model of Microslices will allow big firm capabilities to be delivered by teams of small firms.

Even if you're not a government executive, I hope that an understanding of the dynamics of Microslices in government illuminates what we should expect of our public sector. In addition, many of the obstacles I describe above also apply to executives of large utilities, semi-governmental organizations, and even big banks. If you are coping with a large bureaucracy, the core principles above are even more important to understand. There are already great firms out there that are ready and willing to help.

CHAPTER 6 SUMMARY

○ Microslices—the accelerating compression, automation, and specialization of professional services—requires executives in both the public and private sectors to change the way they buy and use those services.

○ The executives who make the buying decisions for professional services hold the keys to breaking free of the limitations of the old model.

○ As with any disruptive innovation, many executives will need to overcome legitimate skepticism—but not let that skepticism devolve into rigid objection.

○ Common objections to Microslices include writing it off as a younger generation's fad, belief that physical personal connections trump results, and skepticism that advanced technology can replace many types of knowledge work. These objections each have significant flaws.

○ Seven key characteristics typify the Microslices model of professional services as outlined in this chapter—they are the natural resulting operational results of the trends described in part I of this book.

○ The government buyer of professional services is not immune to Microslices, and an analysis of near-term trends in government contracting demonstrates its emergence.

○ The seven key characteristics of Microslices apply equally to private and public sector buyers of professional services.

CHAPTER 7

HOW TO BUY PROFESSIONAL SERVICES

Price is what you pay. Value is what you get.

–Warren Buffet

've outlined the Microslices model of today and the future. I've also given you the principles that accompany that model. Now it's time to put those concepts to work. How you choose a firm, or a collection of firms, and manage them is the most practical function that you need to master.

A word of caution: If you are simply unwilling to accept any model or approach other than the one you are using now, you are not going to like this chapter. Many consulting and professional services firms have grown through alumni networks or similar connections to former employers; that approach will become less effective in the years ahead.

There are near- and long-term considerations when you're ready to identify the right firm and then to manage it. Acquiring advice in the future, say in the 2025–2030 period, is going to be so different that it's hard to predict, so this section will focus on the next ten years. Still, the way that you manage those firms now will help you adapt in the long run.

The Current Professional Services Market: From Lunch Pails to White Shoes

It's important that you have a firm understanding of the consulting market today.

Top-tier consulting and law firms are often called "white shoe" firms—often quite old and established, these firms can hire the best talent from the best schools and can charge exorbitant fees. Another class of professional services firms are what I call the "800-pound gorillas"—giant companies that do everything, from strategy to technology to process outsourcing to body shopping. A third common category of professional services firm is the "boutique": niche market specialists that employ between 10 and 500 workers. Finally, there is a class of professional services firm that I call a "category buster," which are doing things a little bit differently.

If you think of other types of advice service providers—law, accounting, and, in some cases, medicine—you'll see that these categories also apply to them. In fact, the terms "white shoe" and "boutique" are often used to refer to law firms and bankers.

The Marketplace: Four Categories of Professional Services

Type	Example Firms	Typical Employee	Pro Tip
White shoe / ultra-elite	McKinsey, Bain, and Boston Consulting Group; Cleary Gottlieb; Goldman Sachs	Harvard graduates with perfect test scores and incredible networks	Old school but innovative. Incredibly expensive. Can get by on sheer talent. Some are already adapting to Microslices—but they're still expensive.
800-pound gorillas	Accenture, PWC, (part of) IBM, Ernst & Young, Booz Allen Hamilton, Deloitte, Baker McKenzie, Clifford Chance	Everyone imaginable. Programmers, lawyers of all types, MBAs, accountants, engineers, political scientists, former military.	Claim to do almost anything, and quality can vary widely from team to team. Pockets of brilliance. Most susceptible to Microslicing and disruptive innovation.
Boutiques	Cornerstone, Censeo, Brightlight, West Monroe, and many others you might never have heard of	All over the map but often use deep specialists in a discipline or industry	Agility and niche focus makes them best able to take advantage of Microslicing—but most won't without help.
Category busters	Yoi, WealthFront, Betterment, guru.com, McKinsey Solutions, Center for Computer-Assisted Legal Instruction	A thin layer of experienced consultants with a growing group of developers and data scientists. Sometimes a "network" of many small firms or a facilitator of those networks.	These purpose-built Microslicers are approaching engagements differently. Limited impact today but growing fast. Think of them as a Consulting Platform as a Service (C-PaaS).

That last model is where we're really focused.

Category busters are often small and have made innovations on the fundamental model of professional services in a way that, I believe, is going to give them an advantage in the long term. They are generally small firms, and like every other start-up, they might fail for reasons that can't be anticipated. But the ones that survive will dominate.

The Ultimate Rule

There is one overarching rule or, as I call it, the "one law to rule them all." That is: stop buying *firms* and start buying *results*. We will come back to that idea and talk more about how to manage the firms you have.

In chapter 6, I introduced seven principles that accompany Microslices. Now, since Microslices are in their infancy, it's going to be hard to hire firms based solely on the new delivery model. But you *can* use the seven principles to identify consultants headed down that path.

/////////////////// A LOOK BACK FROM 2030 ///////////////////

HUMANS PLAY DIFFERENT ROLES

Even in 2030, humans are still incredibly important (despite premature reports of their doom). Fundamentally, all the technology that we have that is helping us deliver Microslices was developed by human innovation. As you are selecting firms in 2015, you have to consider how you hire firms that are prepared not just for 2015 but for 2020, 2025, and 2030. Which ones are best prepared to adapt their model to help you? Humans are still here, but humans are doing very different things, so it would behoove you to select firms in 2015 that are poised for this change.

//

Checklist for Using the Seven Principles in the Selection Process

It's important for executives to have practical tools to help select firms that are prepared for Microslices. This guide will help you make better choices.

Check #1: Every professional services firm should have a working and increasing understanding of data science and technology.

If you're hiring a firm that focuses on data science, technology products, and solutions, you certainly expect them to have those skills. However, with the development of Microslices, you need to make sure they understand how Microslices affects their *delivery*, not just their *deliverables*.

They need to understand how Microslices changes the way they give you value (not just the actual value they provide) and how a firm relates to technology.

A Microslices-ready firm either understands how data affects their solutions—*or* they need to partner with firms that provide that as part of their engagement.

It's okay if the firm isn't brilliant at the latest in predictive analytics or data mining techniques, but they should know about those things and, importantly, know where to acquire those skills. Ask yourself, if they don't have that ability themselves, how are they getting it? Are they partnering? Do they have joint ventures? Are they part of a "networked delivery model"? Are they "soft-skill people" in partnership with a data science firm or technology firm as part of the joint team? One way or another, every firm must have an answer.

But consider this: Would you want to hire an organizational development (OD) consulting firm that doesn't know how to measure workforce success or change management? If they don't know how to use statistics, data, and technology to deliver all that—and interpret results—they will miss important insights. It's that simple.

In chapter 9 of this book you'll read about a firm called Yoi that is using data science and technology applied to organizational development problems. Yoi is building a platform that delivers the value you might have expected from a leadership coach, but it's using data science and technology to get it done.

IT consulting alone is a $14 billion sector of the consulting market. However, it's shocking how little technology is used *within* firms to enhance the *way* they deliver.

In short, an average consulting firm will sell you consulting. A *great* consulting firm will attempt to replace itself with technology and science. So look for a firm that understands how your particular problem is influenced by technology and how they intend to use technology to deliver results.

How to Use This to Hire the Right Firm

- Read the content of the firm's website, blog, social media, and other publications.

- Read the employees' personal social media streams.

- Are they writing about how they measure and perform quantitative analysis on what they do?

- Ask them about data science used in their projects.

- Ask what kind of technologies they use or what they use to deliver and/or manage projects.

- Look for a firm that is not just thinking about what technology they can sell you but how they use technology to enhance their firm's delivery. (That should also be evident in their proposal.)

Red Flags

- ○ If a firm isn't able to talk about how technology influences them, they probably are not paying attention to the current trends.

- ○ If a firm claims that they focus on "soft skills"— organizational development, leadership training, company morale—and therefore don't need to understand data science and technology, they are likely to miss important insights.

- ○ If a firm makes recommendations only based on experience and doesn't conduct hypothesis testing, they might be subject to decision bias. Do they ever cite or refer to data or encourage you to collect and use it? Or do they just argue very persuasively?

- ○ If they've never even heard the term *data science*, or are not clear on what that means, you might want to look elsewhere.

- ○ If they pull out an abacus or a 40-year-old calculator to figure out how much their fees should be, or if they are sending you emails via Lotus Notes or smoke signals, you might want to look elsewhere.

I do want to underscore that firms should understand the difference between the technology products they can sell you (or tell you to use) and the technology that they actually use and employ to solve your problem.

When I began to share the trends and possibilities that are presented in this book with the executive team at Big Sky, we quickly realized that the firm had to change. We already focused on using data for our clients, but we have worked relentlessly to transform the company into a Microslicer.

To do that, Big Sky created a new line of business called Skysolve™—a catalogue of tools and plug-in services that either amplify or automate consulting activities that previously we completed from scratch each time. We're still advising clients on the same things we were advising them on before, but Skysolve is changing the way we deliver that advice through the use of data science and technology.

Chapter 9 presents a case study on Skysolve and how Big Sky is testing unstructured text analysis in its consulting engagements to accelerate its work and deliver value to clients faster. Bringing this back to Check #1 above, Skysolve is Big Sky's concerted effort both to build a strong internal capability in data science and technology and to present that capability to clients.

Check #2: The firm you hire should be willing to share in the project's risk.

A good firm will be willing to discuss putting their own fees on the line to demonstrate commitment to success. In most cases, value-based pricing (in which the firm is paid on the basis of the measurable value it delivers) or fixed-fee pricing (in which majority of the risk is borne by the firm) are the best ways to accomplish this.

This can be easier said than done, especially in places like the government. (It might not even be allowed. In some cases, there are tight restrictions on what a firm's contracting policies will allow them to do for value-based pricing.) However, even if it is impractical from a contractual perspective, you should still ask the question: "Are they willing to share in the project's risk or not?"

In fact, when you are negotiating with a prospective provider of professional services but may not be able to get those terms approved by your contracting authority, it's ideal to conduct yourself as if value-based pricing will be used then to negotiate your way into a better position. By acting as if every professional services contract is based on value delivered, an executive gains a far better understanding of the provider.

///////////////////// A LOOK BACK FROM 2030 /////////////////////

THE END OF GUESSING

In 2030, even our lawyers (and legal software) demonstrate hard ROI. For example, when you hire a lawyer, aren't you often trying to reduce the probability of some negative result that you're at risk of experiencing, like a lawsuit or catastrophic event? Can you calculate the damage that would occur if those different scenarios played out? If so, can you assign probabilities to various levels of damage? If you can, then your lawyer ought to be having a conversation with you about how to reduce those probabilities from a statistical perspective.

///

Then you can compare the lawyer's fee against the damage that would be caused by different kinds of negative events, and presto, you have a business case for paying that firm. While legal risk calculation is already something sophisticated buyers of legal services are doing in 2015, it's performed by omnipresent apps in 2030 and is a normal practice of every business.

Frankly, most law firms I've encountered would be allergic to value-based pricing, even with the growth in available data and an understanding of outcomes and probabilistic statistics. It's what insurance companies do every day, but it's not a practice that's steeped into the culture of many professional services firms.

How to Use This to Hire the Right Firm

○ Ask the firm directly if they ever contract with value-based pricing or put their fees at risk depending on the outcomes of the engagement.

○ Ask them to provide specific examples of projects where they have delivered value-based pricing and what the results were like.

○ Ask the firm if they calculate the at-risk fee or if you, the client, calculates that fee.

○ If they don't (or you can't) contract with value-based fees, ask for the firm's track record of delivering fixed-price engagements.

○ Don't allow firms—or your own organization—to leave contracts vague. "Other duties as assigned" is not a good basis for calculating value. Be specific, and know what you need and when it's needed.

○ If you're a government buyer, don't give in to pressure to set up time-and-materials (T&M) or cost-plus contracts. These two horrible inventions of the contracting world place the risk almost entirely on the government.

Insider Tip

If the relationship manager at the prospective professional services firm with whom you're meeting freaks out or shows any kind of discomfort or fear, they might not pass this check. The best reason I have heard for why a firm would not provide value-based pricing? They don't trust the client. If the consulting firm doesn't trust you, the client, or there's something about the engagement that's so poorly designed that that kind of question has to be asked, it's probably not a good fit. At that point, the objectives of the procurement should be revisited.

Check #3—The prospective firm's sales, proposal, and delivery should be focused on results, not labor hours and techniques.

All professional services firms should be able to confidently sell to the client based on how they deliver results for value. You should be focused on results that will be delivered, not on where, when, or how the work is performed or even by whom.

You may be asking yourself, "Wait a second, my problem is leadership coaching. You can't measure that! I need their proposal to provide their approach and labor hours in great detail." Just because it's *hard* to measure the final results of the project doesn't mean you shouldn't. Most of the things that you need help for from an expensive consultant are hard to begin with, and by comparison, defining the result clearly should be relatively easy. You should still insist that the firm's sales or business development conversations with you center on value, and focus the engagement design around the outcome.

It's true that quantifiable outcomes can be harder to come by in certain disciplines like team building, cultural alignment, company morale, conflict resolution, and policy development. But consultants should be experts in measuring those things. As such, those themes should be readily apparent in their approach to sales, marketing, and thought leadership.

Take a firm that purports to be a specialist in improving workforce morale. Its marketing material might cite a study with an experimental group, for instance, that demonstrates that a 20 percent increase in morale is directly correlated with a client's revenue and profit. In short, pitches from professional services firms should be based primarily on science and evidence, not conjecture or gut feel. While difficult, and requiring assumptions and nonofficial methods, measuring traditionally "soft" benefits is an absolute requirement in the Microslices era.

What are you looking for? *Results-oriented thinking.* That's critical for a firm that's optimized for Microslices. Furthermore, those firms should understand that there are a handful of beneficial results: cost, quality, time, and flexibility. While there are myriad forms that each of those four results take, every goal of every organization is rooted in one of those types of benefit.

Results are another way of saying "effectiveness." Effectiveness is a function of cost, quality, time, and risk/safety—period.

While I will not get into the definitions of those four types of benefit here, every executive should insist that every professional services firm articulate their delivery results in terms of one or more of those types of result.

○ In the sales process, or proposal process, did the firm ask a lot of questions about the measurable results you want to achieve? If they didn't, they cannot possibly submit a proposal that achieves measurable results that you want.

○ Ask every firm—even the technical ones—how they can help measure intangible benefits like morale, readiness, customer satisfaction, or brand impact. If they don't understand the question, you might need a different firm.

○ If, when pressed, the firm gets even less specific and points instead to the unknowable nature of the universe or quotes motivational posters, you should quietly sneak out of the conference room.

○ If a prospective provider can share specific stories with you about how they've measured success elsewhere, including certain intangibles, then they might be a winner.

Check #4—Any firm you choose should use fixed and value pricing to negotiate based on interests, not positions.

There are many examples of how buyers mistakenly focus on positions rather than interests when choosing a firm, but pricing is an excellent example.

As I mentioned earlier in the book, most of professional services remains dominated by the "tyranny of the labor hour." Most of the proposals I've read say something to the effect of, "We will give you

10,000 hours for this many weeks—or months or years—and all the people we give you will be very smart with fantastic resumes." When laid bare, I hope the absurdity of that approach is clear to you.

An executive could put a whole lot of very bright, very determined people in a room, and it's very possible that nothing good would happen. Throwing a lot of smart, expensive people at a problem does not necessarily *solve* the problem. Smarts without purpose—or a clear result—are unproductive.

The way that a project is estimated and priced is critical to aligning the interests between a buyer and seller. As such, you must hold every professional services firm accountable for that alignment. As Microslices become more dominant, this is an imperative for executives who use consultants and contractors frequently.

> The more attention that is paid to positions, the less attention is devoted to meeting the underlying concerns of the parties.
>
> **–Roger Fisher,** *Getting to Yes: Negotiating Agreement without Giving In*

The root issue of the pricing problem is that professional services firms and clients take the hard and fast *position* that advisors, lawyers, consultants, accountants, and so on should be paid by the hour. And they put this position above the *interest* that they both share, which is the specific desired outcomes. Whether that outcome is cutting costs by a certain amount, completing "the following ten things," or deploying a new process, the outcome is what we should all be focused on.

In the tyranny of the labor hour, pricing is completely out of alignment with both parties' interests. The buyer and seller take a position of hourly billing (or cost plus, or the like) that doesn't make any sense. This is particularly acute if a professional services firm isn't building in an interest in achieving a specified outcome. (See Check #3.)

We can all agree that pricing is important. How a firm prices its products and services also tells you a lot about how a firm thinks about its value. If a firm is pricing by the hour, what they are effectively saying to you is, "We don't exactly know how long we will take, what we are going to do, or what result will be delivered. Therefore, we must charge you on the basis of time." In other words, a firm that wants to price by the hour doesn't have great confidence in what it is going to do or what it is going to deliver. You as the buyer should find this alarming.

Conversely, a firm that charges a fixed price for a specific deliverable or charges on the basis of value is saying, "We don't know how long this is going to take for sure, and it doesn't really matter because we have a mutual understanding that this result is worth "X" dollars to you, and we are going to give it to you for that price." In other words, a fixed- or value-pricing firm knows exactly what it is going to do and what it is going to deliver. Furthermore, they know exactly what that is worth.

Totally different mindsets.

This isn't just a consultant, provider, or advisor problem. Clients who spend innumerable hours of their own time counting and checking the hours their advisors work are wasting valuable resources and only providing their service providers incentives to produce less in more time. Every defense of this approach fails a basic logic test, as shown in the contrasting "perception charts" below.

The first graphic below is a matrix of the consequences of your perceptions of both *effort* and *results* on an hourly billing project. As you can see, the *best-case scenario* is that you get what you expect but your consultant has no incentive to be innovative in delivery.

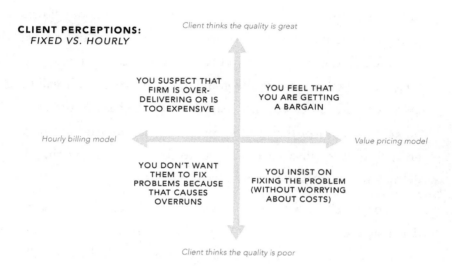

CLIENT PERCEPTIONS:
FIXED VS. HOURLY

Client thinks the quality is great

YOU SUSPECT THAT FIRM IS OVER-DELIVERING OR IS TOO EXPENSIVE

YOU FEEL THAT YOU ARE GETTING A BARGAIN

Hourly billing model

Value pricing model

YOU DON'T WANT THEM TO FIX PROBLEMS BECAUSE THAT CAUSES OVERRUNS

YOU INSIST ON FIXING THE PROBLEM (WITHOUT WORRYING ABOUT COSTS)

Client thinks the quality is poor

The next graphic also shows the consequences of results and pricing, but from the perspective of the service provider.

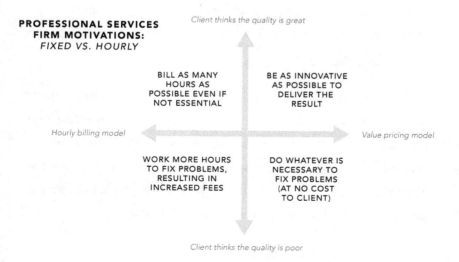

PROFESSIONAL SERVICES FIRM MOTIVATIONS:
FIXED VS. HOURLY

Client thinks the quality is great

BILL AS MANY HOURS AS POSSIBLE EVEN IF NOT ESSENTIAL

BE AS INNOVATIVE AS POSSIBLE TO DELIVER THE RESULT

Hourly billing model

Value pricing model

WORK MORE HOURS TO FIX PROBLEMS, RESULTING IN INCREASED FEES

DO WHATEVER IS NECESSARY TO FIX PROBLEMS (AT NO COST TO CLIENT)

Client thinks the quality is poor

As you can see, the worst-case scenario is that you don't get what is expected and you don't have to pay for it

Nothing could be clearer: "time and materials" projects are a bad idea.

An insistence on hourly billing by a professional service firm probably means that it (A) doesn't trust your company, (B) doesn't know how to deliver value, or (C) is unclear what result is to be delivered.

If the last statement is true, that doesn't mean that you shouldn't work with the firm. It just means that both parties need to work harder to define clear, often more granular, outcomes that the firm feels confident assigning a fixed price to.

For example, Big Sky routinely tells its clients and prospects, "If you can't measure about five times our fee in gained value, you probably shouldn't hire us." This may be an unusual way for a firm to speak to a client, but we are very serious about delivering results and providing value.

Even in situations when Big Sky has no idea how long it will take or what we're going to do, we will say to our prospective client, "You know what? For a fixed price of 'X' we can work for two weeks, and at the end of that two weeks we can give you a deliverable that will tell you how to solve the problem." For government contracts, which can be very hard to predict, we work hard to redesign deliverables and fixed prices as soon as we know there is a change in scope.

○ First and foremost, all professional services require honesty and ethics in pricing for all parties involved. You should not tolerate any lapse in ethics, ever.

○ When selecting a firm, look for one that's willing to talk about quantifiable goals, benefits, or results at the end of the project and is willing to put some of their own fees at risk based on the achievement of those results. A proactive firm will at least be willing to talk about it.

○ If a firm is only willing to bill by the hour, it may be a sign that they are not confident that they can provide the answer you require at the quality level expected in the time available.

Check #5—Using their talent to replace themselves.

Talent is critical, but just as critical is *how* that talent is used when people are providing you advice. Take a look at the "white shoe" firms we discussed earlier—McKinsey & Co., Bain & Co., and Boston Consulting Group (BCG). It's obvious that with their size, reputation, and resources, these companies can hire some of the smartest, most talented people on earth. The people they— and firms like them—deploy on engagements are truly exceptional and well trained.

The challenge of these firms is that they are entirely too expensive to keep around long, even for Fortune 500 companies. This means that they must transfer actionable knowledge to clients—which can be very difficult to do.

Big firms that provide "SETA contracting" or staff augmentation services pose a different challenge. They might use highly talented individuals to get started with a client but are under intense pressure to replace those top people with more junior staff to enhance profitability. That junior staff is less incented to be brilliant than they are to be indispensable. So they often embed themselves in the organization and stay for months—or years (especially in government)—working on the same problem. Executives who are under pressure to keep things going won't be able to do without them and will have to keep paying them the hourly rate in order to stay above water. That's not a healthy relationship.

The really great firms—the ones that are very committed to using gifted, talented people to transfer knowledge to the client so that the client is successful independently—see how Microslices can solve both of these problems and in doing so will facilitate the transition of control and value back to the client.

If you are a consultant or lawyer or accountant reading this book, you might feel skeptical or even alarmed. The good news is that gifted and talented people are constantly coming up with new, innovative solutions. That well does not run dry. People displaced by this phenomenon will shift their productive activity toward functions more suited to advisors—innovation, creative thinking, and facilitating networks of people and technology.

How to Use This to Hire the Right Firm

○ Carefully study the kinds of people a prospective professional services firm hires. Do those hires reflect an understanding of Microslices as we've defined it in this book?

- Look for a firm that has a talent level of people that seems unusual for its size, location, and the years that it's been operating. It's a good leading indicator of that firm's success. For example, Palantir went from 0 to $7 billion in just a few years but did so on the backs of an utterly phenomenal group of founders and early hires. Are they attracting talent that seems like its way out of their weight class? People that ordinarily you would think would only go to a McKinsey?

- Ask them about their hiring process, the things they look for, and how they recruit people. For example, Big Sky goes through a process where we source hundreds of candidates every year and aggressively interview on our core values first, searching for that millennial attitude. We want people who understand the implication that technology is having on data science and how we deliver our results.

Check #6—Insist on measurement.

As I mentioned earlier, just because something is challenging to measure doesn't mean you shouldn't try.

If a firm is adapting to Microslices, its people are going to insist on measurement. They are going to talk about it obsessively. They are going to measure things that maybe even you don't ask them to measure. But agreeing that measurement is the key to success should be a mutual, shared commitment between the services firm and you, as the client.

Many professional services organizations are still "soft-skill" cultures where measurement and quantitative thinking are not something employees are trained for. Many professional services organizations lack a native measurement culture or a data science skill set inherent to the company. Because of this, it's even more important that you make sure the professional services firms you hire are doubly committed to measurement and data. It's a critical precursor to successful professional services engagements. It doesn't matter if an engagement is for process improvement, organizational development, HR consulting, or IT consulting. The consultant needs to understand it, needs to know what's important to measure—and how to measure it.

As Microslices becomes the dominant model of professional services over time—and as these slices get delivered more quickly in smaller components—it will require you to rapidly evaluate results and consider alternatives. If your advisors are not committed to measurement, and perhaps not good at it, you won't be able to measure how well you're doing. You won't be able to determine whether they've been successful. You won't be able to use one of their Microslices when you need it. The whole system falls apart.

In the end, a firm that is thinking about how they are going to use measurement on an engagement is going to give you a better result.

How to Use This to Hire the Right Firm

○ First and foremost, do your homework on every firm you might hire. Read their writing and materials—blogs, tweets, white papers, and webinars. Develop an understanding of how they think about the problems they solve and whether that reflects a measurement culture.

○ Listen to the speeches of the executives, and read their personal social media. See what they talk about and how they talk about it. Find out if they like "quant stuff."

○ Do they talk about the success of their clients in terms of measured numbers? If they do, you might have a winner. If they don't, or if they're vague, you have to start asking why.

○ When they submit their proposal, if it doesn't include a measurement plan, send it back and insist on one, no matter what kind of engagement it is.

○ Ask offerors to explain how they use measurement during the recommendation phase and how they use measurements to influence what they are advising you to do.

○ Dig more deeply into the tools they use to conduct quantitative analysis. Do they have tools and techniques that make it simpler and easier to use data as part of the engagement?

Check #7—No cookie-cutter work but no gold-plated specialization, either.

What Microslices gets you, the executive, is "mass customization"—customized advice assembled from smaller, standardized modules. This benefits you because it's cheaper, easier, and faster.

Current professional services models aren't set up to deliver that way, so executives should be adept at identifying both "cookie cutters" and "gold platers."

The gold-plated model is epitomized by very customized solutions, what I would liken to a hand-tailored suit that's custom-made for your every peculiarity. In contrast, some firms focus on the repeatable delivery of proprietary methodologies so that they can deploy less-experienced or less-skilled resources. Some people would call that approach "cookie cutter."

Microslicing gives clients the best of both worlds while avoiding the worst of either. You should not be subjected to a cookie-cutter solution, but you also don't need to pay for a gold-plated, handmade specialization by a single firm. If the Microslices are sufficiently focused, you get a customized solution for a reasonable price very quickly. A Microslices model allows advisors to provide mass customization without sacrificing specificity. In short, to customize advice, the Microslices model assembles some very small, standardized modules delivered by many firms—this is what Christensen refers to as a "networked delivery model."

Those modules are getting smaller every day and are focusing on narrower slices. Sometimes, they are specified by industry. A truly progressive firm is able to show you how that advice can be broken down into smaller chunks—and how it can be reused, sometimes within your own company. That advice is assembled in such a way that the solution is customized.

Two decades ago, this kind of customization produced on a mass scale was unthinkable. That's because the complexities of assembling a team of professionals quickly—geographically dispersed, with wildly different specializations in numerous firms—were too great to overcome. Now, it's possible to build, for example, a complex process design involving HR, security, technology, and finance using five different specialty firms in a way that is transparent to you. In the end, you get what you need. The key is for you to make it easy for the providers to do that, not harder.

I worked for two of the "Big Five" firms (the largest consulting and accounting firms in the world at the time) during my career. At one of those firms, we were trained on an "enterprise transformation methodology"—a common offering for many consulting firms at the time. Our training manual was excruciatingly detailed. The intent was for the firm to use that on every single engagement in the practice. When you are a big firm and need to create repeatable delivery processes to allow junior resources to deliver more consistently, this is a great idea. It is *not* good if you are looking to deliver a customized approach based on what the client needs.

I am startled with how many professional services firms are too quick to throw a proposal over the wall without an understanding of what the client needs. It is simply impossible to know what will be delivered, when it will be delivered, and what kinds of tools and specialists we might need within our network to deliver the results required without two-way communication.

How to Use This to Hire the Right Firm

○ Evaluate their methods. If a firm has already decided on a methodology for your engagement without talking to you, that's not a good sign. That means they might go down the cookie-cutter path.

- Try to get examples of the firm's other proposals. If they are identical to the one they gave you, they might be pursuing a cookie-cutter approach.

- The way to find out if a firm is going to give you this "best of both worlds" approach is to really examine how they engage with you in the sales process. Do they try to uncover your problems? Or do they start by presenting you with a bunch of PowerPoint slides, telling you how they're going to solve your problem…a problem that they don't know about yet?

- Ask a firm how it can leverage the expertise of other firms, technology partners, and specialists to enhance value. If they claim to do everything in-house or are averse to partnering with world-class partners, you might want to look elsewhere.

Government Contracting or "The Road to Hell Was Paved with Good Intentions"

I would be remiss if I did not highlight the particular challenges of adhering to the seven checks above in a government procurement environment. The truth is that the culture of contracting makes it hard. The good news is that there is serious thought and effort behind acquisition reform, and hopefully the innovative experiments in pockets of GSA, the Air Force, NASA, and elsewhere will prove that there are better ways of doing business.

The old adage that "the road to hell was paved with good intentions" must have been originally referring to the Federal Acquisition Regulation (FAR), which—by trying to eliminate the risk of anything bad ever happening—causes bad things to happen all the time.

There are two things that every government executive must know about contracting for professional services:

1. Fear of mistakes has caused contracting officers and executives to "invent" ethical issues and rules that don't exist. The White House and OMB have been engaged in a five-year-long "myth busting" campaign to correct these false beliefs, but they persist everywhere. The most pervasive (and damaging) of these myths is the belief that government buyers of professional services aren't allowed to engage in communication with prospective firms before a contract is awarded. This isn't just false, it's also incredibly destructive to the public interest.[52]

2. Most contracting officers are fearful of what they don't know and need your leadership to use FAR-compliant, but unfamiliar, contracting techniques. Long-standing practices of using hourly billing, cost-plus contracting, and a host of other "tried-and-true" methods have resulted in the calcification of contracting for professional services. That's particularly destructive when government executives want to procure leading-edge technology or do anything small or anything fast.

The government in particular is saddled with a dependence on hourly contracts despite the White House's best effort to make

52 | Daniel Gordon, "'Myth-Busting': Addressing Misconceptions to Improve Communication with Industry during the Acquisition Process," (Memorandum, Executive Office of the President, Office of Management and Budget, February 2, 2011).

fixed-price contracting the method of choice. At Big Sky, it has taken us seven years to get to a 100 percent fixed-price government contracting model—and the results are astounding.

The cost-plus billing model is even worse than the hourly model. This model is often used in construction, but believe or not, it appears in consulting and professional services too. In this case, a proposal is made and the government or buyer says, "Okay. You're allowed to make a 6 percent profit on this," and the firm is required to deliver it that way. Nothing could be more destructive to both the client and the professional services provider than this system of perverse incentives. Professional services firms are directly incentivized to deliver the bare minimum at all times, while the government is relegated to bean counting and hour watching. If I could wave a magic wand, I would ban this type of contracting immediately, because it's a horrible misuse of taxpayer resources.

The same thing takes place with "lowest price, technically acceptable" (LPTA) contracting in the government. If you are a buyer and you are accountable for a result in your organization that drives mission or profitability or has an influence on the stakeholder—or, God forbid, has human lives on the line—it is an *enormous* mistake to give in to ill-advised lowest-bidder awards. In the end, you are the buyer, you have a lot of influence, and you can influence how those decisions are made. And if you can't exert influence, then you *should not buy*.

I've given you seven specific screens that evaluate how you're hiring a professional services person. I've explained those screens, and I'm giving you specific tips. Now you have a good start on how to choose a firm.

This chapter has presented a guide for an executive to make better selection decisions for their professional services firms. If you take nothing else away from this section, remember the following:

1.   Don't hire based on brand; hire on technical and quantitative savvy.

2.   Insist on clear, measurable results; don't insist on methodology or particular resumes.

3.   Don't pay people by the hour. (Don't do it! Stop!) Do pay fixed and value-based fees.

4.   Don't hide behind policies or regulations; do find a way to focus on the above principles even if rules make it harder.

The next chapter presents practical steps you can take to help you deal with the firms you *already* work with—as well as specific things you can do to improve the performance of your professional service providers in the next year.

CHAPTER 7 SUMMARY

○ Buying professional services is complex; in addition to the three traditional models of professional services firms, a new class of firm is emerging as a result of Microslices that makes it important for executives to rethink how they select firms.

○ To prepare for the emergence of Microslices, The number-one rule for executives is to stop buying firms and start buying results.

○ Using a checklist based on the seven principles outlined in chapter 6, executives can use a seven-part checklist to help improve their evaluation of firms they might want to hire.

○ Check #1: Every professional services firm should be data science and technology literate.

○ Check #2: Every firm should be willing to share risk with their client.

○ Check #3: Every firm's sales, proposal, and delivery process should center on results over methods.

○ Check #4: Every firm should offer fixed and/or value pricing so that their interests are aligned with your interests.

○ Check #5: Every firm should use their talent to teach, not cling.

○ Check #6: Every firm should have a plan for measurement, no matter what field they are in.

○ Check #7: Every firm should offer "mass customization"—a customized solution for your organization based on the organization of a network of specialized offerings from multiple sources.

○ Public sector leaders should be aware that using this checklist will require leadership to avoid cultural resistance—but every single check above is consistent with the FAR and other regulations.

REVITALIZE WHAT YOU ALREADY HAVE

It is the obvious which is so difficult to see most of the time. People say "It's as plain as the nose on your face." But how much of the nose on your face can you see, unless someone holds a mirror up to you?

–Isaac Asimov, *I, Robot*

ompanies and governments are reliant on service providers, and naturally they want to prepare themselves to meet Microslices head on. The great news is that there are a number of professional services firms who really "get it"—and are adopting new methods that will help their clients. The bad news is, most aren't prepared for rapid change and will require their clients' leadership to change more quickly. This places a burden on executives like you.

In many cases, those firms will not change unless you, the client, requests—or insists—that they change. Why? Because, as we've mentioned in previous chapters, they may not yet understand that it is in their own interest.

If you have a strong understanding of how to trigger service provider change, you will achieve far more benefit sooner from Microslices—not just today, but in the future, as you and your consulting providers grow together.

The last chapter outlined what good professional firms should look like in the near term and provides some guidelines on how to change the way you select professional services firms.

This chapter is a little different. If you're like most executives, you have consulting providers doing a wide range of things. Many of these providers are cast from the "trusted advisor" mold and operate in a traditional way, which is in conflict with the checklist provided in the previous chapter. However, their teams are made up of people you've had a relationship with for a long time; like any good leader, you are probably reluctant to change.

This chapter is designed in a question-and-answer format to respond to the queries we hear frequently when talking about Microslices. A top concern: how to manage—and change—the contracts and professional services relationships that are in place. This chapter examines this concern and suggests ideas that will help you steer your current professional services relationships in the right direction.

Since we are talking about the firm that you already trust, I want to be crystal clear before we go any further: *the purpose of this book is not to accelerate or contribute to the failure of your current professional services providers.* The purpose of this book is to make both them and you stronger.

In the best-cast scenario, you get to continue working with the people you know and trust while taking advantage of Microslices. However, research shows that technology-driven disruptive innovation takes down established players with alarming regularity.

In some cases, established firms do adapt well, but it's often because they intentionally attack their own established business model. They essentially go out of their way to say, "We see that there is a new model coming. We are going to change the way we sell and deliver to our current customers even though we know it is going to break our old way of doing business." Quite frankly, most businesses just aren't willing to do that until it's far too late to change. By that time, there will be new players established that outperform the old players by most measures.

As you read, understand that your current professional services relationships can adapt and change. But many need your help in order to make that change. They need you to insist on the changes that are required.

This chapter gives you what you need to identify which of your current consultants is adapting and is likely to be a viable long-term partner.

Now, let's get to down business by answering the most important questions about your current professional service providers in the context of Microslices.

Do I need to cancel all of my contracts?

Don't be hasty. Most organizations should give their partners the opportunity to react. However, most organizations, particularly in government, wait far too long to terminate underperforming services contracts, because of the difficulty of establishing contracts in the first place. If a professional services firm is already underperforming—and you've tried to fix it before you even heard about Microslices—you probably need to cancel that contract.

What can I ask my consultants, contractors, lawyers, accountants, or other advisors to do right this minute?

Three simple steps that help align your contracts with Microslices' underlying principles can be taken with your advisors in one email. Put this book down and write your version:

Karen,

I am delighted with the progress of our engagement so far and expect that it will continue. To help me and the team better understand and communicate how we're doing, please create a simple spreadsheet with the following information:

*First, I'd like a **list of results** you will provide on the engagement by a specified date. Put that list in column A of the spreadsheet.*

*Second, I want to estimate the **value of each of those results**, in dollars. Do this no matter how hard it sounds or unquantifiable you think the results might be; I would like at least a rough estimate. Please include* *what you think the financial or measurable impact will be of qualitative results as well. Put that number in column B.*

*Third, I'd like to understand **the fees associated with each result**. I know we're on an hourly contract, so please estimate what it will take to achieve each result. [If you are on a fixed-price contract, congratulations, put that number right there.] Put that number in column C.*

Thanks,
Bob

A link to a letter and a sample spreadsheet is in the Resources section at the end of this book.

Simply doing this and reviewing it with your advisors regularly will be transformative, even if it's not contractually binding (yet). Maintain this table for every single advisory engagement you have of every type—law, accounting, consulting, HR consulting, and so on. That allows you over time to build a data set of firm results—value and fees that you can use to improve contracts over time. In addition, this approach can become a basis for decision making about which kinds of products and services are delivering value and which are not and what to do about it.

Over time, the goal is to create more granular slices—yes, Microslices—of specific results and associated costs. That way you are armed with info you need to buy those slices again later. Don't worry about how those results are delivered—just about what the results are and how much those results cost. If you ask your consultants these questions, they will be forced to look to technology and Microslices to transform the way they work—because over time that's the only way to increase the value per dollar of fees for clients.

Doesn't it matter what my "consultants" are doing? Some of them are consultants, but some of them are really doing IT work or just augmenting my staff.

It's true that Microslices will dominate the easily automated tasks of a consulting engagement first: activities like data gathering, basic analytical functions, contracting activities, and report creation. Because of that, certain kinds of roles are going to be susceptible to Microslicing sooner; you don't want to be last to adopt an automated version of a very expensive professional service.

For example: structured, repeatable activities like data collection and data analysis will be among the things that are going to be Microsliced first. Highly creative activities like high-level strategy, subjective interpretive analysis, litigation, and graphic design will change later.

No matter what your professional services firms are doing, whether they're "staff aug" (what some people would call "butts in seats") or the most expensive consultants in the world, they should be actively discussing with you how their delivery model is adapting to the trends I talk about in this book.

All of my current providers are on hourly time-and-materials or cost-plus contracts. What can I do to fix that right now?

First, stop issuing time-and-materials contracts so that you don't end up in the same mess later. Cost plus is even worse and lines up every incentive against you. Second, if you can renegotiate the terms of the contracts you have to fixed price, do it. You can use the spreadsheet introduced earlier in the chapter.

You should expect some resistance. Often, "no" is a knee-jerk reaction in an attempt to completely eliminate risk and conflict. You might need to work very hard to explain that fixed and value pricing obviously tilts the balance of risk in your favor. Great in-house contracting officers, attorneys, and accountants understand this and will help you achieve your goals.

If there is resistance from your professional services firm to adjusting the terms, then you need to be concerned about whether they're the right firm. Something is not working. Either the scope is not well defined—and they don't have what they need from you to define it—or there is something more fundamentally wrong with the trust in the relationship.

If you can't change the contract terms, you can simulate a fixed-price contract even on time-and-materials contracts. It's certainly not ideal, but it is better than doing nothing.

Here's how you simulate a fixed-price contract: First, you create charters within the scope of that time-and-materials project. If the project is a long, 10,000-hour-per-year time-and-materials contract, help the firm break the work down into nonbinding but notionally fixed-price deliverable charters, which would fit within the scope of the time-and-materials contracts. Those charters should very firmly state the work, products, or results to be delivered within a specified time—just like our spreadsheet above.

In addition, clear metrics should be defined on those charters for how success is being measured. While you can't specify a binding "price," you can set a budget based on contract terms for each charter.

Ideally, both parties would benefit from coming in under budget. Unfortunately, that's not going to happen often on hourly projects; miraculously, all of the hours will be expended almost no matter what happens. However, make a concerted effort to get closer to associating fees with specific results, which aligns your interest with those of your services firm. Afterward, migrating to fixed-price contracts becomes much easier to do.

What signs might indicate whether my service providers are prepared for Microslices?

The checklist in chapter 7 is a great place to start, but there are two things to watch in any firm: *words* and *deeds*.

First, pay attention to what they say, write, and think. Do your consultants write, speak, or publish? What do they say about data and technology trends? And what do they say about the impact—not just on clients—but on themselves? What is in their proposals and other materials they give to you or release to the public?

Almost all professional services firms are committed to content marketing, which means they write, speak, and talk—a lot. What firms choose to talk about gives you an indicator of *how they deliver* those services to their clients. For example, one large global firm writes extensively about analytics, cloud computing, and a variety of other technology and data science trends that I cover in this very book. They obviously have very bright futurists on staff. However, they write almost exclusively about how they can help clients build solutions and not very much about how these trends change their own delivery model to those clients. It's a critical distinction that, as you review their work, you will understand.

Second, pay attention to what they do when they prospect, sell, and deliver—to your organization or to others. Nobody is surprised when a consultant talks a lot. To cut through the noise, you need to assess the alignment of a firm's words and opinions with their actions on the ground.

Most of the time, the first opportunity for you to evaluate this alignment is during the sales process. Even if you have already hired a firm, you are still in its sales process, because most firms want to grow existing accounts. Does the firm center its sales approach on learning what results you want to achieve and how you want to measure those results? Does it focus on value and fixed pricing in its discussions with you? Does it share how its use of technology can help reduce engagement costs or speed up delivery time?

Pro Tip: If the day-to-day team you're working with is unfamiliar with their own firm's books, articles, or speeches, the firm is not aligned. As I mentioned at the very beginning of this book, just because a firm's great at information technology advice *does not* mean it's great at using information technology to improve its services. When buying professional services, you need to see the delivery of ideas match the ideas themselves.

How can my current advisors start Microslicing? What exactly can I get today?

As I've mentioned, Microslices are already happening. There are three quick hypothesis tests you can conduct (don't worry, they're easy) to confirm that a task could be Microsliced. Any of these conditions make it a good candidate, but the best candidate tasks will pass two or three of these conditions.

1. Does the task focus on a narrowly specialized part of the overall effort or make a part of the project more specialized?

2. Can the cycle time or duration of the task be significantly reduced through innovative methods, including but not limited to technology improvements?

3. Can the task be partially or fully automated?

Here's a hypothetical example of how you might uncover an opportunity to Microslice. Let's suppose that your company, a chemical company, has retained a law firm to be your outsourced general counsel. Suddenly, one of your R&D teams makes a breakthrough and you need to get the intellectual property locked down as soon as possible. Your law firm advises you that while they are generalists, they have a partnership with an IP firm that can do the patent search, which is the first step in the process.

1. A patent search is a very narrow, specialized task within a very narrow, specialized part of the law focused on industrial intellectual property. Check.

2. Patent searches can be cumbersome, and the law firm thinks that—by improving some processes and using API connections to connect to multiple public databases—there might be a way to cut the time to complete a search in half. Check.

3. Currently, one person with the firm has to coordinate with the IP specialist partner to explain the challenge,

send samples, answer questions, and otherwise shepherd the process. A system using APIs and some simple technology could be developed to automate most of the work. Check.

Your law firm, luckily, is staffed with brilliant, Microslicing-savvy professionals who see the opportunity. Within a year, they launch a separate company, which created a technology tool that provides automated patent services to law firms and companies all over the United States. It is routinely delivered as part of a network of service providers focused on intellectual property. Instead of paying them an hourly fee, you now pay a fixed subscription for all-you-can-eat patent work.

On the flip side, remember that software delivered by a services firm is not usually a Microslice. It's software implementation. A necessary condition of Microslices is that a professional services engagement is shortened, more specialized, or automated. If what a firm is providing requires them to provide even more consultants to implement, it is not a Microslice.

What are some other examples of Microslices?

As you might expect, my own firm has developed a range of tools that help us shorten projects, increase specialization, and automate our work. What you'll notice: a lot of these tools are built with plain vanilla technology, while others are more advanced. It's not the tech that makes the Microslice—it's the result. Here are just a few examples from Big Sky's experience:

- A cloud-based diagnostic application that replaces voluminous and expensive in-person interviews with remote automated interviews and surveys.

- An Excel-based model for forecasting demand in a process.

- A slider-model build on Google Sheets that replaces budgeting guesswork by automating "what if" analysis on budgets.

- A structured text-mining algorithm that helps us save time in document review by recommending focus areas based on node analysis of PDF files.

- A cloud-based analytical platform that replaces manual data collection and analysis for assessing and analyzing a federal agency's insider threat posture.

Our clients didn't hire us to deliver any of these tools that meet the Microslices criteria—in fact, we have never sold a piece of software or a tool to a client. These are Microslices that help us compress, specialize, and automate the consulting services that we are already providing to clients. The results are the same (or better); the method is different.

The key about Microslices is that it doesn't have to be a cloud-based Hadoop app that's looking at a two-terabyte data set (although it might be). But it does need to compress, specialize, and automate the consulting basics to be a true Microslice.

I have a long-term, trusted relationship with my current coach/consultant/lawyer/accountant. Doesn't that count for something?

It most certainly does count. Be aware, however, that trust will diminish in importance over time in many knowledge worker relationships, because many more knowledge worker functions will become increasingly commoditized. Trust is simply a factor that people are willing to trade time or money or quality for. As price drops, quality increases, and timelines are shortened, trust will take a back seat to results. This is not new; it's a big reason why Indian outsourcing firms have performed well and have been acquired by many US professional services firms.

For the moment, trust still matters, because that trust will allow you to separate winners from impersonators. Right now a trusted advisor is going to be upfront with you about whether his or her firm is in a position to adapt to Microslices. A trusted advisor will even be honest with you about another solution that replaces him or his advice.

How do I know what to pay for a Microslice? I just found out what it is when I picked up this book.

The best way to price any services project is to ask yourself what a successful result is worth in dollars. Period.

Among the best on this topic is Alan Weiss, who has been writing about fixed and value pricing for a long time. Back when

I was a midlevel consultant, he changed my thinking completely about how to deliver value to clients.[53]

In the end, if you know that a particular solution is worth a million dollars to you, you really shouldn't care how much labor is required to achieve that result. You shouldn't really care about how it gets delivered.

Imagine that a home builder offered to build you a new home for $300,000 in one year. Another builder offers to build the house in only nine months for $320,000. That is a tough decision that depends on our personal circumstances. However, what if a third builder offered to build the same house in a week for $400,000?

I don't know about you, but I'd probably be skeptical of the third offer—unless the contractor could prove identical quality. A house is complex, and it would be hard to be sure that you'd get the same result. However, for small, specialized professional services projects, you can measure and validate the result. If the example above were a consulting project, would you still be skeptical? Even worse, would you want to pay less because there are fewer labor hours for the house built in a week?

As a buyer, I challenge you to reject those who would decide how much a project is worth based on the labor that's required to complete it. If one firm can deliver a specified result in 6,000 hours for $1 million, why would you want to pay less if another firm can deliver the same result in only 3,000 hours? Rejecting a firm for being twice as efficient just doesn't make sense. The

53 | Alan Weiss, *Value-Based Fees: How to Charge--and Get--What You're Worth*. San Francisco: Jossey-Bass/Pfeiffer, 2002.

bottom line is that you should understand what a successful result is worth to you before you hire a firm.

What about project management? Do I as the buyer need to change the way I manage my consulting firm support?

The answer is yes. At Big Sky we focus carefully on project and program management—and the cornerstones of communication, governance, and measurement remain critical. That doesn't change. However, what happens within those cornerstones changes—for you and for the firm you hire—when you Microslice.

Adapting Project Communications for Microslices

Communications in Microslices projects will change, because there will be fewer on-site team members. Instead, a more diverse set of specialists will deliver the result. The focus of communications will also change, from "project status" and activity updates to communications centered on results, value, and time. The client employees involved in consuming those Microslices get different kinds of communication. You might not have to warn your team, as you may today, that an army of consultants will arrive to interview them. You don't really have as many consultants in the meeting, because the Microslices model doesn't require those advisors to be on site.

Adapting Project Governance for Microslices

Governance is the way decisions are made on a professional services project by both the team and the client. When you're managing a services provider, how do you make a decision based on the advice they give you? How do you decide to tell them yes or no? Much of this will change in a Microslices environment, when results and transparency are crystal clear to everyone involved (and without the need for a lot of PowerPoint slides). In many organizations, governance is as much about authority and persuasion as it is about measurable results. The Microslices model affords the opportunity for you to adapt decision making to a faster cadence, using automated tools. There are challenges, however—as networks of small firms and individuals band together to quickly solve a problem, governance of their interaction will likely be beyond the client's direct control.

Adapting Project Measurement for Microslices

Needless to say, measurement is critical for any project management process. With its focus on results and value delivered, the Microslices model requires a deeper commitment to measurement.

As an executive, it's critical for you to understand how you plan to measure success. Otherwise, your professional services firms will not be able to measure their progress against those results. In many engagements, it's already hard to break through the opaque processes your professional services firms use—it would be unwise to compound the problem by being unclear on the measurable endgame.

In addition, Microslices shifts project measurement from a complex array of utilization, hourly burn, and estimates to complete, to a cleaner focus on the outcomes and those variables that most influence the outcomes. Rather than chasing a lot of what Eric Ries[54]

54 | Eric Ries, "Why vanity metrics are dangerous," December 23, 2009, http://www. startuplessonslearned.com/2009/12/why-vanity-metrics-are-dangerous.html

would call "vanity metrics," you and your consultants can focus on fewer, better measures that really matter.

Questions You May Be Thinking, but Probably Shouldn't Say Out Loud

My consultants are Microslicing already and figured out a way to cut their team size in half and deliver the project three months earlier. How much of a discount should I ask them for?

This is where you have a cup of tea, contemplate your life, and ask: "Why do I care?"

If you are getting the result you want from the best delivering Microslices to accelerate your success, you have to stop asking questions like that. If you want a discount from a service provider, you need to ask for it at the beginning—not after the project is completed.

I'm used to seeing the employees of the firm I've hired in the office all the time, so I know they're working all day. Won't I lose that?

Just because people show up at the office doesn't mean they're effective. Several years ago, Big Sky adopted a model called a "Results Only Work Environment." In short, it means that "work is something you do, not somewhere you go."[55] Our team

---

55 | Cali Ressler and Jody Thompson. *Why Work Sucks and How to Fix It: The Results-Only Revolution.* Portfolio, 2010.

members are accountable for their own time and schedules and enjoy unlimited vacation. We do not ask people where they were yesterday or what time they're coming in on Friday; in fact, it's against the rules. Instead, our people commit to achieve specific results by a specific time, for either our firm or our clients. As long as those results are met, they have complete freedom to work when and how they see fit.

Our managers do ask questions like, "We have a deliverable for the client due on Friday. Do you think you will be able to get it done?" It's a very different question. Many firms have adopted practices like ours, which are ideal for a professional services firm that is embracing Microslices and fixed or value-based pricing.

Sometimes, of course, delivering value requires a physical presence. If one of your consultants needs to run a facilitated session, obviously they need to be in the room. If an attorney is supporting you in sensitive negotiations, he or she may need to be with you to adapt to a very rapidly changing real-time problem. Just remember not to let the tail wag the dog: showing up doesn't create value; doing the right thing the right way at the right time creates value. The more you focus on results, the less you need to worry about babysitting your professional services firms. It also helps establish a stronger relationship with your providers.

> I don't really like the way my consultants
> are [insert activity here].

Are you worried about what you're getting, or are you worried about how it's getting done? Does it matter whether they're using Macs or PCs? Does it matter whether they are conducting interviews with a software tool or in person? It may. But it isn't worth the worry if the results are being achieved. It's crucial that firms have the flexibility to be innovative by using automation, tools, and other methods to adopt Microslices. Micromanaging methods will halt progress in its tracks.

If you focus your oversight on results and interim results, you're going to have more success adapting to Microslices. Those methods are going to become more automated over time, so you'll be able to measure results much more quickly. In short, do not let style trump substance.

My consultants are doing work on "soft" problems like culture and leadership. Does Microslices apply to them?

It does. It is very important that the buyer holds such firms accountable for applying data science and technology. Without it, you may be making very big decisions based on gut feel and guesswork.

I'll share an example of how my own firm has replaced advisors with Microslices. Years ago, we paid an outside coach to interview all of our employees, administer a proprietary survey, and interpret the results. Afterward, this coach would provide a nice, shiny binder full of the results and provide us with rec-ommendations. We were definitely getting the results we were looking for, but when an opportunity arose to automate—and improve—this process for lower cost, we jumped at the chance.

Today, instead of using traditional methods, we use an automated tool and process provided by a West Coast company called TinyPulse to measure culture and other human capital factors. Instead of someone coming in and interviewing everybody and giving me feedback once every six months on how everybody is doing, the entire team gets weekly input on specific questions as well as the opportunity to provide feedback and suggestions. It's not only cheaper, faster, and easier than the old way—it's also more effective.

That's not to say there isn't a time and place for leadership coaching; there is. However, the focus of that coaching will become narrower over time—and will rely less on people. As leadership and cultural consulting and other soft disciplines become more susceptible to Microslicing, top firms will be forced to specialize in automation.

What legal and/or regulatory barriers do I need to worry about?

In the short term, government and highly regulated industries will be more constrained in their ability to adapt to Microslices. This is particularly troubling for essential government services and defense, which cannot afford to lose ground.

It's not news that it takes these organizations longer to adapt. Fortunately, there are pockets of excellence working hard to adapt. For example, the General Services Administration's 18F is charged with helping agencies overhaul how they buy digital services—and 18F has been at the forefront in helping agencies rethink how they undertake contracting.[56] Today, contracting officers in the government and procurement officials in highly regulated industries like

56 | Jack Moore, "GSA wants to make it easier for agencies to buy agile," January 8, 2015, http://www.aptac-us.org/news/gsa-seeking-greater-agility-contracts/

banking, energy, and healthcare need to be thinking about how to conduct low-risk experiments in their companies and agencies to prove (to their attorneys and regulators) that procuring Microslices is possible and far more effective.

In the long term, every industry will be challenged and pushed beyond what they think is possible. Our regulatory structures, while necessary, are completely and woefully unprepared for the coming change.

You've talked about many firms delivering together and the "networked delivery model." I use multiple firms now—is there benefit in pushing them to work together on deliverables right away?

Probably not, unless they are already equipped with the tools and techniques of a mature networked delivery system.

Open APIs and other technologies, along with old-fashioned partnerships, will enable networked delivery to happen faster in the future. However, you should not be in the business of organizing or administering that delivery network.

Why? Because you are an expert in your business and the problems facing it—not the organization of a complex system of companies, specialists, and technology solutions. Your number-one job is to understand what you need and what your problem is. This is why most competitive bidding processes are so flawed; they often are so saddled with rules and requirements that they have the effect of engineering artificial teams of professional services firms.

It's not in your best interest to try to become an expert in designing a networked delivery model; it is the natural consequence of organizations like yours insisting on results and professional services firms naturally organizing in the most efficient way to deliver those results. As the Microslices model grows, providers will emerge who specialize in assembling those networks—and the process will be relatively transparent to the buyer.

How do I write a RFP (Request for Proposal) or SOW (Statement of Work) using Microslices?

The flippant answer: RFP processes are usually ill conceived and poorly executed, in both the public and private sector. However, since it's a fact of most of our lives, you need to use them as effectively as possible.

In the pre–Microslices model, RFPs often don't allow sufficient communication between buyer and seller. This prevents the right specialists from working with you to clearly define outcomes and results. In short, the RFP creates distance between the entities that need to be closely connected. This is often done in the name of fairness. But it is often taken to extremes and well beyond what is required.

For now, when you write an RFP, focus on the seven principles outlined in this book. Specifically, be sure to include a careful and precise definition of the results you want, when you need to receive those results (if you are time-bound), and any constraints or limitations that may be in place on how those results are turned over. Finally, you must continue to insist on firms providing references and qualifications from other clients that prove that they can deliver what they claim to deliver.

In summary, write the RFP to focus on the "what" and the "why"—not the "how" and the "who."

By doing this, you will dramatically improve the quality of the responses you receive from offers. Instead of pages of canned marketing materials and claims of "customer centricity" and "best in class methodologies," you'll get candid, brief, and clear explanations of what is to be delivered, the value of that solution, the timing, and the price.

Adaptation of Current Relationships Requires Commitment

In the Resources section at the back of this book, you'll find two handy checklists—one for working with your current provider and one for choosing new providers. (You'll also find a sample of Microslices that Big Sky offers, just to get an idea of what to look for.)

The key question you need to be asking of your current consulting engagements: How do you cultivate an approach, culture, and mindset that allows your company to stay relevant and thrive as Microslices emerge?

There are things you can do today that will put you on a future-minded path for success. The Resources section at the back of this book is filled with practical tools that will help you get started right away as you start to change the culture in your company to prepare for this shift. I also provide you with a reading list that will help you stay at the forefront of this movement so that you and your company can remain relevant as the culture around us shifts.

Before proceeding to the case studies section of this book, take a moment to reflect on your professional services contracts. Make a list of all of the providers and the tasks they're performing for you.

Now imagine that you could compress every single one of those tasks by 50 percent. Imagine that every single result listed in the next column could be provided with 50 percent less time and effort. In that scenario . . .

○ *What would change (not just about those results but about your advisors and your relationship with them)?*

○ *What are some possible outcomes unrelated to those results that would be positive?*

○ *What are the results that would be worth making a change in your culture or current structure to achieve?*

○ *What are some outcomes that your team or your employees might view as positive about this?*

○ *What are some things about this scenario that might be challenging? (They all sound like they're going to be great, but my guess is that some of those changes may be quite uncomfortable at first.) What do you do about that?*

○ *How might all those things, if they happen over a sustained period of time, change your company culture?*

CHAPTER 8 SUMMARY

○ As important as it is for executives to change the way they select their professional services providers, they must also take action with current providers to adapt to Microslices.

○ Organizations that are willing to work with their professional services providers to adapt have an excellent chance at success, provided that both sides are committed to change.

○ The most important shift for managing your current professional services contracts is to shift the focus of the contract from activities to measurable results.

○ In the short term, executives can work within their current contract structures—which may not be ideal for Microslices—by establishing nonbinding charters within tasks that help you and your providers understand the results to be delivered and by when and what value those results will deliver.

○ In the long term, executives should work with their professional services partners to lay the groundwork for new contracts that accommodate the seven principles outlined in chapter 7.

○ Strong governance, communication, and measurement remain the cornerstones of good project management, but the nature of each will change to reflect the more automated, rapid, and networked delivery model of Microslices.

CHAPTER 9

CASE STUDIES

Where we're going, we don't need roads.

–Dr. Emmett Brown, *Back to the Future*

The first eight chapters of this book showed the forces changing the consulting industry, why the Microslices model is the future of advice giving, and how you can react to it. But you need examples of how executives have solved real problems. The case studies in this chapter provide examples of Fortune 500 companies and government agencies that have chosen to do things differently. And these stories will also help you understand how the Microslices model can be applied. More importantly, they demonstrate how a few organizations are ahead of the curve and in the best position to adapt to change.

yoi

CASE STUDY #1: A FORTUNE 100 TECHNOLOGY COMPANY USES A UNIQUE "REAL-TIME SENSOR SYSTEM" TO REPLACE TRADITIONAL COACHING AND CONSULTING.

A Fortune 100 company,[57] which we'll call *Yorkle*, had a problem. As one of the most successful tech firms of the last 20 years, it relied on hiring the very best engineers in the world. However, it found that after years of growth, it was losing top engineers at a high rate—especially newer hires.

Executives found that Yorkle's onboarding process wasn't uniform—and in some places was nonexistent. Exit interviews with departing employees revealed that their experience was damaged by poor onboarding practices. For example, one software engineer didn't get a laptop for a week. Another didn't know where to sit. Yet another didn't know who his manager was. Thus, people were leaving too soon after the company had spent tens or even hundreds of thousands of dollars on hiring and training.

Of course, engineers don't "grow up" with onboarding skills. Managers in an enterprise like Yorkle are promoted for world-class tech skills, and knowing how to bring on a new employee doesn't come naturally. However, for a top-tier tech leader, onboarding is the point of most influence with a new employee.

---

57 | This book can't mention the name of the company because of the sensitive (and embarrassing) nature of the problem.

Many organizations faced with a problem like this feel the need to turn to the outside for help. They might hire an HR consultant or a lean operations firm with experience in personnel or a strategy firm employing former chief talent officers at leading technology firms. They may have brought in management consultants and perhaps "ideated" a bunch of "best practices." Once that consulting firm was finished, the company would receive PDF documents that might be the basis of training. At best, they'd keep some of the consultants around to give them a hand; at worst, they'd post it to the company intranet and hope for the best.

The Solution: Yoi: a real-time sensor system for onboarding.

Instead of hiring a consulting firm, Yorkle turned to a quirky start-up called Yoi, the brainchild of former Deloitte CMO and

KEITH FERRAZI

author Keith Ferrazzi and Tony Hsieh, CEO of Zappos.com.

For Yorkle, Yoi provides a SaaS that measures workers and the way they interact. By collecting data in a simple user interface across meaningful categories of human behavior, Yoi delivers justin-time information about why onboarding is (or isn't) going well. Just as Fitbit[58] collects leading indicators on physical health, Yoi collects leading indicators on onboarding health. The data collected isn't haphazard—it's based on extensive research on human behavior.

For Yorkle, Yoi delivers a series of scripted "assignments" for workers that creates interactions, which are measured by the Yoi platform. Yoi watches how that script unfolds and, through observations of everyone in the process, measures what's going well and what isn't. The scripted assignments might be typical onboarding activities like "meet with your onboarding buddy" or "manager meeting," but instead of continuing down a specified path, Yoi dynamically changes assignments based on the results of the interactions between people. It then creates a network of trusted assessors in the company and drives new interactions that allow assessment of 40 or more categories of onboarding success. Assessments might be "how well does the new hire know the product?" or "How well does the new hire understand our core values?" The assessors' responses to those questions change what happens next in the onboarding process.

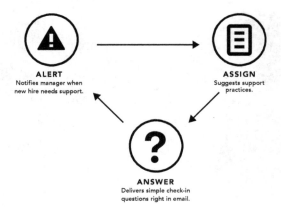

ALERT
Notifies manager when
new hire needs support.

ASSIGN
Suggests support
practices.

ANSWER
Delivers simple check-in
questions right in email.

---

58 | Fitbit (www.fitbit.com) is a wearable activity tracker that allows healthy people to be geeks, too.

Unlike traditional survey instruments or coaching, however, the results of those interactions and assessments create triggers that immediately determine the next appropriate assignment. Instead of waiting for a feedback meeting, Yoi tees up the next best action. For example: if the new hire doesn't understand a product, that data is delivered back to the Yoi platform. Yoi then creates a new assignment for the employee regarding the product on which he or she is weak. In turn, the results of that new assignment are fed back into the platform.

How it benefits the executive

It's hard to calculate how many billable coaching or consulting hours Yorkle has saved by turning to Yoi instead of a coaching or consulting firm. But many other benefits are clear. What's more, as data is collected within the company, the marginal value of each use of Yoi increases.

First: Yoi compressed the time between the observation of an onboarding gap and action or intervention in the onboarding process—shortening that time frame reduces stress, fear, poor performance, and misalignment.

Second: Yoi reduced variation in the onboarding process. Yoi clarifies the process and its branches, defines clear, consistent intervention "assignments," and collects micro-level data that provides ground truth to the manager.

Third: Yoi reduced the "time to productivity" for new hires. Fast moving tech companies cannot afford for top new-hire talent to sit on the shelf for two months while they get acclimated—they need them producing and right away. Among Yoi's top hard benefits to Yorkle is reduction in time to productivity.

Finally: Yoi—when compared to what would be required in time and resources consumed by traditional professional services firms—reduced the cost and time to fix the onboarding problem. By using data science-backed tools in a platform that automates the advice-giving process, Yoi accelerated many specialized functions that would be performed by a professional services firm.

How it demonstrates Microslices

Yoi isn't out to disrupt the consulting industry. But it is replacing a function that consulting and coaching companies perform—optimizing the onboarding experience for incredibly expensive employees. The president and chief products officer of Yoi, Larry Hitchcock, calls it "telemetry on people in the enterprise." Yoi is designed to radically compress the feedback loops that occur during onboarding, using data and technology that makes it easy for managers to take action.

All this is not just to drive better onboarding for employees; it also builds better managers and creates consistency in the enterprise.

Yoi's invention was driven by questioning how companies conducted and improved onboarding. Until recently, the approach to improving the onboarding process was driven by hours and hours of specialized personnel conducting coaching, consulting, and training. That approach is very difficult to scale and difficult to replicate, and even if you get it right, it's hard to know if the improvements you've built are sustaining themselves.

Yoi uses concepts centered in data science, technology, and culture explained in part I of this book and applies them to the improvement of the onboarding experience. It is based on applied data science (specifically, behavioral data science) by driving KPIs to the micro level, not just the macro level (as might be typical of consulting) and using the science to measure, verify, and manage cultural change. Its technology profile is based on cloud-based delivery and large-scale data aggregation. Finally, Yoi's quick adoption by customers is an example of how millennial thinkers are quick to adopt technology that augments and strengthens personal and professional connections.

Hitchcock says that the future of Yoi will be driven by the ability to leverage more data about what behavior matters and in turn using Yoi's automation to support those behaviors. As that future unfolds, Yoi's specialized offering will further automate and compress the improvement of onboarding for very large companies.

CASE STUDY #2: HEWLETT-PACKARD USES AN ORGANIZATIONAL INTELLIGENCE SAAS PLATFORM TO AUGMENT PROFESSIONAL SERVICES AND ATTACK CAPACITY CONSTRAINTS.

Tech giant Hewlett Packard (HP) is a $112 billion business. Price aside, data collection and analysis to solve operations problems is a necessity. HP provides one of the most comprehensive sets of information technology products and services on the planet. The world's second-largest provider of PCs, HP also sells servers, storage devices, printers, and networking equipment—on top of HP's expansive services business.

One of HP's major businesses was not meeting financial expectations. HP knew that it had to find out why—and fast. Specifically, the executives knew that the business was facing serious capacity constraints that had a direct impact on financial performance.[59]

The Solution: Automated capacity management analysis by 9Lenses

To tackle the capacity problem, Hewlett Packard partnered with a Microslicing firm called 9Lenses. The goal was to collect raw feedback from HP employees and uncover hidden capacity constraints. Typically, this raw feedback collection would be performed via interviews or simple surveys.

APPROACHES TO UNCOVERING HIDDEN CAPACITY CONSTRAINTS

ACTIVITY	ANALYSIS: Breadth & Depth	COSTS: Resources & Time
HP'S USE OF 9LENSES	✓ High	✓ Low
STRATEGY TEAM INTERVIEWS	✗ Low	✓ Low
DETAILED WORKLOAD MODELING	✓ High	✗ High
CONSULTING ENGAGEMENT	✗ Low	✗ High

Source: 9Lenses and CEB

9Lenses created a framework for HP on its SaaS platform, which augmented how consultants collected and mined data from everyone in the business. Unlike a typical survey, this diagnostic

59 | "Quality Snapshots," Corporate Executive Board, Arlington VA, 2014

included broad, open-ended questions that allowed for unfiltered feedback from respondents.

For example: respondents were asked questions like "What wasteful activities are commonly observed but rarely mentioned (in other words, the 'elephants in the room')?" In turn, respondents were provided the opportunity to submit as much input as appropriate. These questions weren't canned—they were customized by the HP team. In fact, HP or any consulting firm can build their own questions and frameworks on the 9Lenses platform to drive automated insight.

The structured and unstructured data from respondents was analyzed by 9Lenses to identify the most critical areas of need, using such applications as word mapping and context-dependent issue scores. These were translated into action-oriented conclusions such as "unclear accountabilities lead to duplicate efforts" or "teams not maintaining swim lanes"—issues that led to overlap and competition that was draining valuable capacity.

The data showed the percentages of respondents who brought up each issue and mapped it into easily digestible illustrative stories, rather than spools of data. In short, with almost no human interaction, 9Lenses collected and analyzed data about the capacity constraints and identified several top issues to address—and delivered it in an easy to understand format for executives.

This story isn't all about automation; in this case, a mix of machine smarts and human touch was critical to a successful outcome. The senior leaders gathered for half-day workshops to develop solutions to the issues that were uncovered. Acting as a guide, a strategist from 9Lenses helped the leaders refine their solutions, bringing them the top employee-generated ideas from the responses. If leaders got stuck during the sessions, the strategist was able to draw additional ideas and solutions from the diagnostic to get things rolling again. While 9Lenses automates some functions traditionally performed by consulting firms, it has become a consultant's best friend by enhancing the speed and value of what those firms can deliver.

How it benefits the executive

According to a thorough study conducted by the Corporate Executive Board (CEB),[60] working with 9Lenses allowed HP to reduce the time it took to collect the data, process it, and determine solutions by about 75 percent. Where the traditional method took 12 weeks, the crowd-sourced diagnostic process took three weeks—a significant measurable improvement. HP's Rob Dzoba said, "The leadership team that received the results said this was the most comprehensive strategy presentation around a business they've ever been part of. It will be the model for all of the regions moving forward."

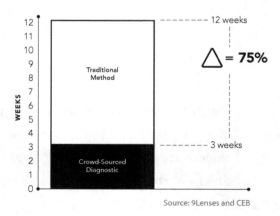

TIME SPENT ON DATA COLLECTION AND ANALYSIS

Source: 9Lenses and CEB

60 | "Capacity Snapshots" Corporate Executive Board, Arlington VA, 2014

The benefits are impressive on their own merit, but the story doesn't end there. The technology allows more and more data to be collected and analyzed over time. HP can regularly use 9Lenses to measure the issues related to capacity constraint—and accelerate learning and corrective action. Several times now, 9Lenses has been used instead of expensive consultants to solve similar problems at HP. Querying across the 9Lenses platform ensures the right questions are asked and responses structured in a meaningful way, while using software collapses the learning process from weeks of interviews to around an hour.

EDWIN MILLER

How it demonstrates Microslices

Like other companies described in this book, 9Lenses isn't out to disrupt the consulting industry; in fact, CEO Edwin Miller's vision is to partner with clients and the right kind of consulting firms. He doesn't just want to deliver a killer SaaS; he wants to help great consulting professional services firms stay great by enabling self-disruption.

I talk a lot about the future in this book, but this is not the future. 9Lenses is right now.

CASE STUDY #3: SALLY HOGSHEAD TRANSFORMS HER TRADITIONAL PROFESSIONAL SERVICES FIRM INTO A MICROSLICER.

While researching *Microslices*, I have had the pleasure of talking to executives who both buy consulting services and sell them—from operations improvement and corporate strategy to branding, marketing, and human resources.

Much to my surprise, I am met with the most skepticism from professional services firms in two particular fields: creative services (such as advertising) and organizational development (such as leadership development). As a result, I feel that it's important to tell the story of a company that has met with success in those fields. Meet howtofascinate.com.

Just four short years ago, Sally Hogshead, owner of How To Fascinate, had a very difficult choice to make. She had a clear, well-developed company philosophy and service offering, a great team, and solid clients. How To Fascinate, both before and after its transformation, has been in the business of "helping organizations and the people within them uncover their most valuable traits."

At that time, her firm was delivering original and high-quality work and adhered to what Sally calls a "Fabergé egg" strategy, which promises a one-of-a-kind experience. Her teams used foam boards for her clients to present ideas, very much like what you might see on *Mad Men*. While technology was available to accelerate or improve delivery, How To Fascinate was somewhat resistant: high tech didn't provide the "artisanal" feel that might be expected of a great creative professional services firm.

Sally realized that this approach of providing advertising, branding, and marketing advice was keeping her from sharing her team's brilliance with a much larger audience. By "larger audience," she didn't mean two or three more clients a year—she meant *hundreds of thousands of people all over the world.*

The Solution: Replicate and automate the delivery of personal branding

SALLY HOGSHEAD

Sally made a decision to change course toward an accelerated and automated delivery of the firm's ideas. She told her employees and long-standing clients that if an engagement didn't line up with the new strategy—requiring the replication and automation of advice—the company would not take the work. Instead, How To Fascinate would shift its focus to building things that were extraordinary and replicating and automating those very few things.

She morphed the company she'd built away from advertising and into the business of building brands for humans—*and doing it in an automated way.* At first, they used the Fascinate tool as a giveaway, but almost overnight, customers—both individuals and companies—saw the tremendous value of rich advice. The tool took off.

In no time—literally in a single day—How To Fascinate was able to provide branding advice to a thousand individual people. And when they saw the possibility of scale and of exposing these ideas to a much larger audience, they doubled down on automation. They did this not just by building a nifty tool but by automation that *replaced* traditional consulting services that branding and coaching consultants provided before.

Specifically, How To Fascinate replaces traditional advice with an incredibly intricate data and analysis engine in the back end that the customers don't see. If you have taken the Fascinate personality profiling assessment, you know that there are 49 distinct types of personalities out there—each of them valuable in their own way with distinct character traits, both advantageous and challenging.

To achieve the promise of Microslices, the company needed to automate the creation of these 49 profiles. It wasn't enough to just automate the collection of survey data on each of the 49 dimensions; to accommodate every individual who might take the assessment, the service also needed to automate the analysis and presentation of the hundreds of different unique combinations possible. Finally, the delivery style needed to match the person: each of the final reports needed to reflect the personality type and preferences of the individual. How To Fascinate didn't just want to automate the data collection and the analysis; it wanted to automate the construction and presentation of results that were consistent with the individual's style and preferences.

To facilitate this, and to remain true to her high-quality feel, Sally drafted months of video scripts so that every single video advice component is tailored to the individual who received it. Based on the diagnostic, How To Fascinate's analytic engine selects different videos and compresses them into a single seamless response, tailored to the client's preferences, as determined by profile traits. In the customized reports, which include charts, copy, and custom video, Sally herself presents the findings. For every one of the styles, her outfits are different. Her tone of voice is different. Her speech is different. The copy is different.

Even after you've taken this survey and you've received the advice, you continue to get customized, tailored advice from How To Fascinate over time. That's because the How To Fascinate system remembers who you are and what your style is and can hypercustomize every communication to fit your unique personal brand. If you've purchased the assessment, you're now a client. Every email you get is tailored to the results from your assessment. The net result is that it feels like you're getting intimate coaching advice, but it's completely automated.

How it benefits the executive

The other case studies in this section talk primarily about the benefits to buyers of services. But in this case I want to highlight the benefits to the consulting firm—because only when both buyers and sellers realize what's possible will Microslices begin to dominate professional services.

How To Fascinate experienced the normal growing pains of a firm transitioning into a new business model: once they got traction, the benefits accrued rapidly. After How To Fascinate's first marketing push with the new model, they made $100,000 in a day. That's when they realized, "Hey, this probably works."

How To Fascinate, and Sally Hogshead's personal brand, has since taken off. The firm has embraced automation in a way that is as crazy as it is creative, as proactive as it is productive. As exceptional as results have been, the benefits to her customers has been even greater.

Sally has had one goal for her clients: to provide one-to-one quality advice to every single person who takes the assessment—which, if you're a traditional organizational development or advertising firm, would be impossible to do for hundreds of thousands of people per year.

How To Fascinate's clients get the gold standard for personality assessments. And they get it without having to bring in a coaching company to conduct interviews and diagnostics with their team, without waiting for a report that is delivered as a PDF, and without needing to schedule meetings with every assessed employee for feedback purposes.

You can now get the deliverables at a level of richness and detail that you'd expect from a leadership coach. The difference is that you can get those deliverables right away. *Right now.* Not ten minutes from now but right after you finish that assessment.

Finally, it's more cost effective. How To Fascinate charges only $15 per person for 2,000 people and up, including the personalized video coaching and follow-up reports and emails. I know of large organizations that spend hundreds of thousands of dollars—even millions—for comparable results.

How it demonstrates Microslices

Sally's company nailed each of the three pillars of Microslicing:

1. *Specialized* on her core professional service—which was the "science of fascination"

2. *Automated* the delivery of that service to clients using data science and a mix of relevant technologies

3. *Compressed* the timelines for delivery so that clients could get results almost instantly instead of months

Her success also shows how Microslices is an important partnership between technology, data science, and people. It lets machines do what machines do well and leaves humanity to the humans. That means How To Fascinate will still go in and do events for clients to help them figure out how to deploy their methods in their organizations.

Everything else, however—everything she *can* automate, while maintaining the same quality level that she would deliver personally—she *will* automate. Every single thing.

CASE STUDY #4: A DEFENSE COMPONENT AUTOMATES A COMPLEX INDEXING ACTIVITY IN PARTNERSHIP WITH BIG SKY ASSOCIATES AND TASTE ANALYTICS

In the wake of large-scale data leaks and growing concerns about protecting sensitive data, a defense organization came to the following conclusion: some lapses were related to the training and skills of its frontline security personnel.

Many security managers said they lacked the proper tools to excel in their responsibilities. For instance, audits found that many security managers didn't know how to respond to the most critical incidents. That's because they didn't know whom to contact when incidents took place and what responses were most appropriate.

To fill this critical security gap, the agency needed to index and "rate" its security positions in order to assign a level of training for these individuals.

The challenge was daunting. For the agency to read, analyze, and interpret thousands of security positions, the workload of just the first stage added up to approximately 2,500 person hours of work, most performed by expensive contractors. For example, just one position description analysis that takes 60 minutes might cost the government $160. If 10,000 descriptions require analysis, that might mean spending $1.6 million to complete the work—on a single topic like security. That excluded the time required to aggregate the analysis, brief it, summarize it, and otherwise make it useful. It was likely the effort could cost the government several million dollars.

More importantly, failure to address the training issue represented a significant risk to the organization of information loss, security lapses, or, worse, potential safety risks to employees. In short, there is risk that there are security managers that don't have the right training or skills to do their job. The thousands of hours spent on indexing the positions would be time not spent on other critical initiatives.

In the past, an agency facing this challenge would have three choices:

1. Buck up and do the work, devoting the valuable time and resources of the agency's employees to complete the task.

2. Hire a contractor to do it manually (more expensive than using the agency's employees).

3. Hire a consultant or contractor to find a new approach to accomplish the task, perhaps coming up with a new process for assigning the ratings or outsourcing the work.

The Solution: Unstructured text analysis
replaces time-consuming reading

Working with Big Sky and a small start-up analytics firm called Taste Analytics, the organization is now exploring a fourth option—a Microslicing approach that automates the work that would be done by those consultants or contractors.

To accomplish this, the team is training a computer to assign the ratings in a fraction of the time it would take a team of humans. Taste provides a UDA (unstructured data analysis platform) that doesn't just crunch numbers; it applies machine learning and artificial intelligence to unstructured text problems to uncover new insights.

For example, imagine that when evaluating security position descriptions, there are three levels of "security rating": moderate, high, and critical. Those ratings are relatively subjective judgments made by people who are experts in security. As you might imagine, the difference between ratings may not be so clear-cut, requiring that a specialist read each description and make a judgment call on whether it constituted a rating of moderate, high, or critical. Pretty mundane and time-consuming stuff, especially if your security specialists have better things to do.

To solve the security position description problem, Taste Analytics' engine ingests a set of keywords that represent security rating levels and trains itself to look for those keywords in a position description. The algorithm that Taste built to solve the problem starts out with a low level of accuracy, but as users, or "model trainers," provide feedback on how it's doing, artificial intelligence kicks in, and the tool teaches itself to do a better job. This functionality makes the tool hungry for data. The more it ingests, the more it learns and the more accurate the model gets.

Now instead of executives seeing a stack of position descriptions with ratings assigned to them, Taste's analytics engine can output charts of how the position descriptions fall on a map of the different security ratings.

Once it's fed, the engine outputs an assigned rating (moderate, high, or critical) and, say, a percentage indicating how "sure" it is about the answer. Depending on the complexity of the position description, the accuracy of the rating will vary, but even outputting a guess at the rating with a low confidence level is valuable—it allows the agency to focus its valuable time only on the small percentage of position descriptions that are most problematic.

AUTOMATION OF REVIEWING TEXT REDUCES CONSULTANT WORK TIME BY 70%

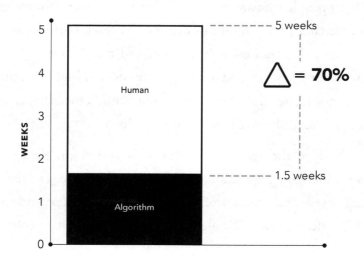

Taste Analytics provides a product to its customers that's lightweight, easy to use, and extremely powerful. It even delivers visualizations for customers so that they can quickly plug it into presentations and analysis and board meetings. This engine can comb through thousands of descriptions in minutes and is scalable to vast data sets—and it does it without the need for a structured format for interpretation, unlike traditional statistical models. As founder Derek Wang explains, "Using deep machine learning algorithms, our engine is able to statistically identify the themes, topics, and emerging issues from any data set without using taxonomies."

How it benefits the executive

The program is still under development. But the government has shown that it's possible to work with a professional services firm to deploy solutions, which replace the same—but much more expensive and time-consuming—work other professional services firms have provided.

First, it addresses a critical security issue that puts the government's information and people at risk: misaligned security manager training. In addition, by avoiding placing the burden on security professionals, their time is freed to focus on more critical activities.

Second, Big Sky and Taste's approach to the position indexing problem will save time dramatically, both for Big Sky and for the government.

Third, the government is avoiding spending scarce taxpayer dollars to have contractors read thousands of pages of position descriptions. As we mentioned earlier, the cost to do it with highly paid professional services is millions of dollars (just for the security positions). By automating large portions of the analytical work, the government has the opportunity to focus human labor only on a small percentage that require additional attention.

How it demonstrates Microslices

The Taste–Big Sky experiment is an example of how a professional services firm can augment or automate its services through a technology platform. Partnerships between companies like Taste and Big Sky are providing executives the ability to use Microslicing to automate and compress timelines on unstructured analysis.

This case demonstrates how a team of professional services and technology specialists can form an ad-hoc network of expertise and capability to solve a narrowly focused problem.

It also illustrates how automation can dramatically improve a function that, until recently, we believed only a human contractor could do.

In addition, the case study demonstrates the Microslicing idea that specialization, not generalization, will dominate future consulting models. You don't need to spend $50 million on some giant, integrated, gold-plated, does-everything product suite from a single firm. That's not the way to buy software, deploy tools, or hire a consultant anymore.

Finally, this is a solution that has the potential to change an agency's culture. As we discussed in part I of this book, a millennial attitude is a necessary precursor to Microslices. The Taste–Big Sky approach isn't driven by human interpretation of documents; instead, it's driven by an algorithm. That algorithm teaches itself how to improve and is rapidly earning the trust of its users. As more managers accept machine analysis, the culture of consuming automated advice will change. That shift is particularly critical as a model like Taste's gets more and more accurate; from narrowing down the positions from 30 percent to 20 percent to 2 percent, more trust in the machine is necessary to realize the full benefit.

To be sure, the solution in this case doesn't completely replace the role of an expert. But it makes those experts far more efficient. By completing the easy work—and highlighting the tasks that are going to be the hardest to perform—the tool can help experts work with maximum efficiency.

CHAPTER 9 SUMMARY

As these four case studies illustrate, there are things that you could be doing now.

- ○ **Case Study 1:** Yoi is helping a leading technology company transform its onboarding process by automating activities that might ordinarily be performed by coaches or consultants.

- ○ **Case Study 2:** Hewlett-Packard used an organizational intelligence SaaS platform called 9Lenses to augment professional services and attack capacity constraints.

- ○ **Case Study 3:** How To Fascinate, a small creative firm, which specializes in HR and personal branding services with almost no employees of its own, used Microslices to build a delivery tool that allowed for exponential growth of the company. It automated the delivery method of giving advice.

- ○ **Case Study 4:** A defense agency working with Big Sky Associates and Taste Analytics is indexing and analyzing position descriptions automatically to both increase efficiency and address an important security gap.

CONCLUSION

There are risks and costs to a program of actions. But they are far less than the long range risks and costs of comfortable inaction.

—John F. Kennedy

While the future of consulting and professional services is hard to predict, we can do our best to arm ourselves with knowledge, tools, and techniques to take action.

One of the best books I've read in the last few years is *Antifragile* by Nassim Taleb.[61] The author argues—in a delightfully combative and cantankerous way—that those of us who pretend to know how complex systems work, or who believe that we can predict the future with great confidence, are wrong. According to him, we can't. There's too much moving around.

He argues persuasively, however, that if we create systems that are decentralized, adaptive, and respond well to chaos, we stand a far better chance of success. Large bureaucratic systems will tend to fail. Whether that bureaucracy and calcification is in the professional services or in the firms that buy those services, it's a recipe for disaster.

61 | Nassim Nicholas Taleb, *Antifragile: Things That Gain from Disorder (Incerto)*, Random House, 2012.

NASSIM TALEB

Taleb's observations are one of the inspirations for this book. The Microslices model is one that is designed to make both professional services firms that embrace it—and organizations that seek it—"antifragile." Firms that are building their offerings around this will make you more successful. Firms that don't face stagnation and irrelevance.

In part I, this book defined Microslices as the compression, specialization, and automation of professional services activities:

It described how Microslices is poised to become the dominant model for those services over the next ten years. In addition, part I provided a detailed, evidence-based argument of the trends shaping Microslices:

1. The accelerating sophistication of data science.

2. Three critical technology developments.

3. The rise of millennial culture.

Part II of this book described the future of Microslices in detail over several stages of development, from 2015 to 2030:

○   Microslices today are solutions to relatively simple, straightforward problems that your advisors can solve using tools as basic as a Microsoft Excel but can also be lightweight, adaptive technology solutions that apply insight to data.

○ By 2020, firms that adopt Microslices will make rapid gains by automating many routine consulting functions. They will benefit from an explosion of specialized applications, new sensors, and sources, connected by open APIs.

○ In 2030, Microslices will be the dominant professional services delivery model. Not only will even unstructured and creative functions be automated, but your computers and machines will be able to assemble, on their own, Microslice networks to dynamically solve unforeseen problems.

Part II also provided you with very clear guidance, not just on how to hire the right kind of firm but on how to manage the firms you already work with.

We presented a framework for selecting a consulting firm based on seven traits or attributes that we think are essential to a firm that is adopting Microslices.

1. **Statistical and technical literacy**

2. **Shared risk**

3. **Results orientation**

4. **Negotiation of interests, not positions**

5. **Planned advisor obsolescence**

6. **Insistence on measurement**

7. **Mass customization**

Part II answered questions on how to make the most of your current professional services partners while also preparing those relationships for Microslices. Your trusted advisors, the great firms that you believe in now, must adapt; they can't make it without your help.

Finally, this book provides a Resources section—with practical tools that you can download and use right now to help you deal with the change presented by Microslices.

Even if you are uncomfortable with this new way of doing business, you can reach out to good firms that find purpose and passion in helping executives navigate the future. A good firm will help you bridge the gap and be your partner in the journey ahead.

This book may have confirmed some of what you already know. It may also have presented contrarian or controversial ideas that challenge your views—or even create a tinge of fear. A little fear can be a good thing; it can motivate you to act and help you identify—and confront—the most important threats to your organization.

After all, courage isn't the absence of fear; it's the willingness to act in spite of it.

As a buyer of professional services, you have the responsibility to spend your organization's resources wisely. I hope you now have a better understanding of why it's important to change the way you buy such services—and even change the way your partners deliver those services.

If we—both buyers and sellers of professional services— embrace the challenge of adaptation, we will engage in unexpected and exciting partnerships to solve the hardest problems faced by our organizations.

What's required? Action over comfortable inaction.

ACKNOWLEDGMENTS

A few individuals have been incredibly generous with their ideas and time, and without them I would have had neither the motivation nor raw material to build this book. In particular:

Leif Ulstrup, for coining the term "Microslices," his exceptional mentoring skills, and for his ability to jump-start my thinking about just about anything.

Keith Ferrazzi, Larry Hitchcock, Sally Hogshead, Edwin Miller, and Derek Wang, for providing their incredibly valuable time and insight into real-world applications of Microslices.

John Bly, John Culbertson, Robert Fish, Manoj Malhotra, Tim Whitmire, David Redding, Scott East, and Adam Witty, for sharing their wisdom on writing and authorship.

Manoj Malhotra, John Miller, Steven Smith, and the Big Sky team, for supporting my efforts to run a company and write a book at the same time.

Lawrence Cruciana, Jason Silverstein, Dan Jodarski, the Advantage team, and everyone else who read, re-read, and re-re-read parts of this book to prevent me from making an ass of myself.

Everyone in Entrepreneur's Organization (EO) for being my coaches, conscience, friends, and mentors.

RESOURCES

To augment this book's usefulness to the executive buyer of professional services, I have posted several useful tools, templates, and checklists for download. You can find this information at www.microslices.net.

1. Microslices Readiness Assessment

2. Model Statement of Work

3. Microslices Value Calculator

4. Current Firm Evaluation Checklist

5. Call to Action Letter to Current Providers

6. New Firm Selection Checklist

7. Government Contracting Checklist for Microslices

8. Essential Reading List

FURTHER READING

1. Clayton M. Christensen, Dina Wang, and Derek van Bever, "Consulting on the Cusp of Disruption," *Harvard Business Review*, October 2013.

2. Erik Brynjolfsson and Andrew McAfee, *The Second Machine Age: Work, Progress, and Prosperity in a Time of Brilliant Technologies.* W. W. Norton & Company, 2014.

3. Salim Ismail; Michael S Malone; Yuri van Geest; Peter H Diamandis, *Exponential organizations: why new organizations are ten times better, faster, and cheaper than yours (and what to do about it).* New York: Diversion Books, 2014.

4. Cali Ressler and Jody Thompson. *Why Work Sucks and How to Fix It: The Results-Only Revolution.* Portfolio, 2010.

5. Peter Thiel. *Zero to One.* Crown Businesses, 2014.

6. Clayton Christensen. *The Innovator's Dilemma: When New Technologies Cause Great Firms to Fail (Manage-*

ment of Innovation and Change). Harvard Business Review Press; 1997.

7. Nassim Nicholas Taleb, *Antifragile: Things That Gain from Disorder (Incerto)*, Random House, 2012.

8. Pew Research Center, "Millennials in Adulthood: Detached from Institutions, Networked with Friends," March, 2014.

9. Ray Kurzweil, *The Singularity Is Near: When Humans Transcend Biology*. Penguin, 2006.

10. Roger Fisher and William Ury. *Getting to Yes: Negotiating Agreement without Giving In*. New York: Penguin, 2011.

ILLUSTRATION CREDITS

○ Clayton Christensen P. 28: Licensed under CC BY-SA 2.0 via Wikimedia Commons - http://commons. wikimedia.org/wiki/File:Clayton_Christensen_World_ Economic_Forum_2013.jpg#/media/File:Clayton_ Christensen_World_Economic_Forum_2013.jpg

○ John Glenn p. 41: Source photo courtesy Wikipedia Commons, https://commons.wikimedia.org/wiki/ Category:John_Glenn#/media/File:John_Glenn_Portrait.jpg

○ Steve Jobs p. 41: Photo by Matt Yohe, used under Creative Commons license.

○ Nate Silver p. 41: Photo by Randy Stewart, used under Creative Commons license.

○ Peter Thiel p. 41: Photo courtesy TechCrunch50, used under Creative Commons license

○ Ray Kurzweil p. 77: Source photo courtesy Michael Lutch, used under Creative Commons license.

INDEX

A

M

N

sensors, 41, 42, 43, 69, 70, 85, 92, 115, 116, 117, 120, 124, 125, 229

Shared risk, 137, 143, 229

sharing economy, 78

Silver, Nate, 39, 48, 237

Singularity, 20, 21, 90, 115, 236

Singularity University, 20, 90, 115

Siri, 85, 123

Slack, 84

Smith, Adam, 32

Software as a Service (SaaS), 205, 209, 210, 213, 226

specialization, 20, 24, 31, 32, 38, 53, 64, 95, 115, 122, 128, 131, 146, 168, 169, 187, 224, 228

staff augmentation, 165

Statement of Work (SOW), 198, 233

statistical literacy, 42

statistics, 44, 46, 49, 59, 117, 151, 156

strong AI, 51, 75

T

Taleb, Nassim, 227, 228, 236, 238

taste analytics, 219, 221, 223, 226

Thiel, Peter, 39, 237

time and materials, 163, 183

Toffler, Alvin and Heidi, 23

trusted advisor, 13, 36, 37, 75, 105, 178, 189

tyranny of the labor hour, 136, 137, 143, 159, 160

U

Uber, 81

unstructured data analysis, 117, 221

unstructured text analysis, 154

US federal government, 139

ABOUT THE AUTHOR

John M. Dillard started his career at the Central Intelligence Agency (CIA) and has dedicated every working hour since to helping organizations, private and public, uncover secrets to stay ahead of future threats—whether those threats are competitive, operational, or security related. His 15-year career in management consulting has benefited everyone from large players such as Deloitte Consulting to smaller companies such as the one he cofounded, Big Sky Associates. His consulting experience runs the gamut: from commercial strategy to government security operations and large scale IT, from banking administrative flows to analyzing operations at the 9/11 recovery site at New York City's Ground Zero. He has written for the President's Daily Brief (PDB), served as a reserve intelligence officer in the US Navy, and has frequently taken out the trash for his own company. He's tough to surprise but easy to keep energized.

When John isn't working on your toughest challenges, he is busy serving his community as a board member of the Entrepreneurs' Organization, a member of Young Entrepreneur Council (YEC), and as a workout leader for F3, a fitness and leadership organization. He is a proud South Carolina native and lives with his family in Charlotte, North Carolina.

For more information about Big Sky, visit:
www.bigskyassociates.com

Printed in the USA
CPSIA information can be obtained
at www.ICGtesting.com
JSHW012024140824
68134JS00033B/2857